Change Course

**One Lady's Race from
Acceptance to Adventure**

Leslie Jackson

2020

"Leslie utilizes her life story and experiences as motivation and fuel to help you overcome obstacles to achieve success in life and work. She invites you into her life with authentic storytelling and real life examples and illustrations. Her goal is to truly help you live your best life ever."

– Dr. Jermaine M. Davis
Professor of Communication and author of
Leading with Greatness!

"*Change Course* is one woman's journey of self acceptance, growing in faith, listening to the Holy Spirit, and knowing all things are possible with God as your guide. Spirit filled and truly inspirational."

– *Colleen Baldrica author of* Tree Spirited Woman

"Leslie Jackson is an overcomer and her life long quest for love and acceptance led her to a miraculous relationship with the One Living God. *Change Course: One Lady's Race from Acceptance to Adventure* is her beautiful, vivid testimony to God's love and amazing grace."

– Jasmine Brett Stringer
Speaker, on-air lifestyle expert, and award-winning author of Seize Your Life: How to Carpe Diem Every Day

"With *Change Course*, Leslie brings inspiration, resilience, and faith to the starting line. Her story has you sitting on the edge of your seat and turning the page faster than you can actually read. We are all in the race of our lives daily, and being prepared to win is a game changing course. Once we realize that, we can make our own dreams come true and success can truly be found. It's the journey that we prize above all else. Bravo Leslie, your race isn't over."

– Pam Borton
Women On Point: Partner & Owner
TeamWomen: Founder & Board Chair
Empower Leadership Academy for Girls: Founder
Author of On Point: A Coach's Game Plan for Life, Leadership and Performing with Grace Under Fire

Change Course
Copyright © 2020 Leslie Jackson

All Rights Reserved
Printed in the United States of America

No part of this book may be reproduced in any form or by any means, electronic or mechanical, including photography, recording, e-books, or any information storage and retrieval system, without permission in writing from the publisher.

ISBN 978-1-7345854-0-7

Cover Design and Chapter Illustrations by Lacey Winchester
Interior design by Sue Stein

For information:
LadyRacing.com
Leslie@LadyRacing.com

I thank my talented, artistic daughter, Lacey Winchester, for her inspiring chapter illustrations and for her cover design collaboration with Sue Stein who also arranged the book formatting.

Dedication

To my mother, Joyce Ella—and to God, my Father,
who has always loved me unconditionally.

I thank you, God, with all of my heart for taking on all of my sins.
I dumped a great load at your feet, but you never once complained.

Table of Contents

Introduction		1
Chapter 1	The First "Telling" of My Story	5
Chapter 2	Spotted in the Neighborhood	11
Chapter 3	Parent Swap	21
Chapter 4	Scott Goes to Heaven	31
Chapter 5	Marriage	41
Chapter 6	Motherhood	47
Chapter 7	Health and Addiction	55
Chapter 8	Light in the Darkness	63
Chapter 9	Dreams Come True	79
Chapter 10	Racing Towards Joy	89
Notes		97
Acknowledgments		99
Author's Bio		101

Introduction

Many times, actually many years, in life I have dealt with adversity which I overcame by digging deep and grabbing hold of the potential I know is there *if I only trust*. My childhood disease made me look like a red-spotted leopard, causing people to stare and make fun of me—leaving me with low self-esteem. Because of this disease, very early on I overcame various trials, instead of curling up in a ball and giving up, I chose to push past the pain I felt when being teased and became strong instead. I learned through trial and error that when we trust ourselves, accept love from others and most importantly accept the love from God, we will get through the dark times and enjoy a life that is abundant and waiting for us.

Another tough lesson I needed to learn was when I thought I was doomed to hell for my sins of my divorces—and that *I was beyond forgiveness.* Yet God showed me this was not true. After years of struggling to love myself, God chose to show me he loved me in a miraculous way by healing me twice. Because of the love He demonstrated to me, I was compelled, even felt called, to write this book about my experience. I hope by reading my story, others will learn to accept the past, learn from the past, find forgiveness, and move forward into the best version of themselves.

My whole life, including the writing of this book, *has been a process releasing that shame.* It did not happen overnight. Because I was able to forgive myself for the divorces and find acceptance, I was able to live without the shame and find joy. Letting go of the shame and accepting who I am has been freeing. I truly feel like chains of guilt have fallen off my hands and ankles. Occasionally during low times I doubted if there was a God, but I am now 100 percent convinced there is a God because He showed his glory to me during the healings. What joy I feel knowing that I am loved, even though I have sinned.

My message is for all. *God's love is not for me alone, you can take hold of it too, if you are willing to seek God and accept the love He has for you.*

With God at my center and no longer feeling weighed down by sin and low self-esteem, I was able to give life to my smoldering ember, my spark, and dare to believe racing could be for me. I always wanted to race cars, but never believed it would come true so I let this little smoldering spark stay in my gut—until one day when the smoldering spark caught fire. I told my husband Jim that I would love to race a car, and we talked about different options. He mentioned his friend who had race cars, and offered to talk to him and get some ideas. Because I gave life to my desire to race through talking about it, eventually the day arrived that I was going to race a car. My car racing has now continued for seven years. Sometimes I lost big, sometimes I was in the top five, and twice I won first place. Was I always racing perfectly? No. Was it fun every time? Yes!

Life is not all doom and gloom, and we need to experience its full glory as much and as often as possible. God did not create the mountains, lakes, trees, flowers and wildlife to be viewed from the cheap seats in the stands, we need to get out and enjoy life to its fullest.

- What healthy desire haven't you given life to that burns deep down inside you that won't go away?
- What is smoldering in your belly?
- What desire, what spark is burning to get out?

It starts with a spark. Let your spark come to life and start that business, learn how to swim, race a car, climb a mountain…you name it, give it permission to begin, believe in your potential, make a plan, and then put the pedal to the metal and enjoy the adventure!

Chapter 1

The First Telling of My Story

> *"This is the first time in my life I have shared my whole story with anyone."*

One day a few years ago, I saw on Facebook an audition call for a theatre show called, *Hard for the Money: Stories of Women, Work & Satisfaction.* I felt like it was calling out to me to submit my life's story. I needed to put my story in a six-minute essay format for the audition.

My life story in six minutes? That seemed hard to do. I sat down at my computer and typed. I typed without any deep thought, and I just typed the words that wanted to get out. My story felt like it needed to come out of me, and I was finally giving it permission. It flowed out effortlessly, it was so easy and it took only about six minutes to type the six-minute essay.

I emailed the producer, stating my interest in her show and requesting to set up an audition. She emailed back and stated she would like to meet me and gave details for a meeting at a local library. I practiced reading my essay several times at home, timing myself to make sure it was six minutes long. It was titled: *Emerging Butterfly.*

At the library, we introduced ourselves to each other and chatted easily. Sally told me about her show. This was her first show; thus she was not able to offer any payment if I was selected. She had a form she wanted me to sign, allowing the taping of my story. I did not know if I could tell my story, and definitely did not know if I could sign a form saying someone could tape my story. I said I needed to think about it. She asked if I wanted to read my essay for her or what did I want to do. I decided to go ahead and read my essay to her and then decide what to do after that.

I stood up and said, "This is the first time in my life I have shared my whole story with anyone." Sally looked at me with compassion and patience. She did not say anything, but she gave me time. I needed to think. Did I really want her to know my story?

I took a deep breath and began.

"My brother was killed in a car crash," I read and had to stop. *I don't know if I can read this on a stage in front of hundreds of people, I thought.* I took another deep breath and repeated that first line. "My brother was killed in a car crash." I continued. When I read the part about being teased about my spots, my eyes threatened to tear up. I stopped, took another long, deep breath and began reading again. Sally's eyes had tears in them too. Her face was soft, full of empathy.

"That was beautiful," she said. I was relieved it was over. "Thank you for sharing. Even if you don't read it with us, it's a story you need to tell others. I have others to audition and then I will get back to you in a few of weeks."

After a couple weeks Sally emailed me asking if I wanted to sign her form and be considered for the show. I thought long and hard about her question. I finally decided to sign the form and returned it to her. After she received the form back she responded that she wanted me to be one of the women on her show. The stories would be read on the stage of the newly renovated Parkway Theatre in Minneapolis.

I was scared to tell my story on stage. Why do I want to tell my story? Or was it that my story needed to be told? Can I hold it inside of me any longer? I opened the gates already by writing the essay, how can I push it back in? The weight of it had been bursting to come out for a long time. I decided it needed to continue its journey out of me and into the world.

Sally scheduled a rehearsal to practice our essays and get to know the nine other women that would be on stage sharing their stories of discrimination, prostitution, personal growth and triumph. The day arrived for the rehearsal in the basement of a library. I was happy we would be meeting in the basement because it felt private in a windowless room. Before we got started, Sally told us she was giving us as a gift, photos of the event and wanted to start that morning with photos of all of us together. So before we were to read, we needed to go back up into the light of day and look happy while photos were snapped.

Back downstairs in the fluorescent lights after the photo shoot we took turns getting up in front of the other women and read our essays. I was to go fourth. I listened to the others tell their stories and wondered how I would stand in front of them and spill my guts. This was so much worse, so many people in the room, compared to when Sally and I were alone the first time I read the essay. As the others read their stories, tears were flowing from many of us as we heard the hardships they had lived through.

At last it was my turn. I stood up, slowly walked to the podium and looked down at my papers. I could not look at the women. I did not have any confidence in my ability to share my story in front of these women. My tears flowed uncontrollably. *How can I do this? I can't tell them my shame, embarrassment, and the tragic death of my brother,* I cried.

Finally, I pulled myself together by focusing on the paper, the words and not thinking about the actual details of my story. I wanted others to know why I was sharing my story. I began, "One thing I'd like to do before I die…" I told them I wanted to make a difference in this world. The women looked at me without judging, they also had endured much and understood. Sharing my personal story with these women and hearing their stories gave us a special bond. We all were survivors in our own way.

The night of our big performance at the theatre it was raining outside and very dreary. We sat in the first row of the theatre with the audience behind us. This time I was eighth in the lineup so I had time to hear the other stories again and watch how it was done. I felt normal—my new normal—the one who had told my terrible story and survived. I was now stronger because of it. I felt confident. I was going to read my story. It was going to be fine, the worst was behind me.

I went on stage and made it through the whole essay without tears pouring down my cheeks. After the show, people thanked me for sharing my story with them.

I realized then that perhaps it was time to write a book. A book will last a lifetime and more. A book can be read by many people and help many people. *I want others to know they are not alone.* Many of us have adversity that we are dealing with and feel like no one understands, but the opposite is actually true. We can help each other. I want to share my story of low self-esteem and how I overcame it. I want to share my story of sins and how I felt it would surely lead straight to hell—and now I know it's not true, I am forgiven. There is so much in the pages of this book I want others to know—they are full of potential, and they too can become stronger and live a life full of joy.

Even with a calling in my heart to write this book, I still felt reluctant to move forward in the process. I kept telling myself, *"You aren't good enough, you have no talent."* Even though I felt God was calling me, my self-doubt kept knocking me down, stripping me of the confidence to accomplish anything worth doing, even if He ordained it. Daily I would ask God to show me the way.

Recently I was reading *Grit: The Power of Passion and Perseverance* by Angela Duckworth where she wrote how our talent can be the very thing that distracts us, preventing us from reaching our goals. After reading that, I realized that God had put the book in my hands—and this has been freeing for me. It's humbling to admit that I have spent my entire life searching for my talent. I can stop looking now because *whatever the Lord anoints me to do* at any given time, for *He is the one who enables it,* plus a sprinkle of my passion and perseverance is all I need for the sky to be the limit.

In my search, I continually sought God for guidance, and not long ago I heard Him whisper into my heart that I was to write about difficult things in my life, that it may bring another person hope. I asked God to give me courage to share my feelings in order to impact the hearts of others.

Until recently I have felt like I have been hiding behind makeup, long sleeves and long pants, stuck in a chrysalis of my own making. With my sugar addiction behind me, and my spots nearly gone, I feel free, I can finally let my skin show and wear the clothes I want and choose whether or not to wear makeup.

The toughest thing was believing my sins were forgiven. *In the Bible it says that all is forgiven when we confess our sins and ask for forgiveness!* I believe Jesus died for everyone's sins and all is forgiven!

Now that I am finally convinced of this truth, God is helping every step of the way as I am emerging from my chrysalis and becoming a butterfly. I love my new freedom, spreading my wings and soaring to unknown heights with purpose! My new journey has just begun.

You now know I survived and thrived, but the rest of my story from little spotted girl to this point is important to read so you know the real me, my struggles, and how much effort I put into reaching this point where I could confidently stand on a stage and tell my story.

Chapter 2

Spotted in the Neighborhood

"We left and got into our van and drove to a nearby store and Mom bought me a stuffed toy, a Dalmatian with spots just like mine."

Drenched with perspiration, my mother's cotton dress clung desperately to her skin in the unforgiving summer heat. With a whale of a pregnant belly full of new life, Mom and Dad headed to the hospital to relieve her of the freeloading passenger she'd been carrying for more than nine months. As the fourth child, my birth was rather ordinary, with two notable exceptions. I weighed in at over nine pounds, living up to the reality of my pre-birth perception as a beluga whale. And as the first and only girl in the family, they rejoiced over my birth, though it only added to the challenge my mother faced with three active, mischievous boys.

Ours was a working middle-class family who lived in a two-story house with a two-car garage in Keokuk, Iowa, and went to the Church of All Saints every Sunday. Mom stayed home with the four kids and tried to keep my three brothers out of trouble as best she could. My brother Scott, at age four, managed to unlock the front door and run out of the house naked, then climbed up a neighbor's ladder so he could play on top of their house. Trying to keep three hyperactive boys out of trouble was more than a full-time job for Mom.

Some houses have those hook-and-eye latches that are cheap fixes for bathroom doors with broken locks; we had one at the top of the front door frame to keep my brothers from escaping while Mom was taking care of me. It became clear that small, clever boys could in three seconds flat use a broom handle to push the hook up and out of that little metal loop and run free.

Dad worked in the engineering department at a local corrugated box company. When he came home from work I would follow him into the bedroom where he would take off his tie and empty his pockets. My hand would be extended waiting for the warm coins he would place into my palms. I would give him a hug and then happily run off to my room to put them in my piggy bank.

As I began to grow, I developed red spots all over my body that looked a great deal like hives. I appeared much like a leopard, only with red spots and maybe I was not nearly as adorable as a leopard. No one ever came up to me and said, "Your spots are so cute. I love them!" Instead, everyone stared, rarely asking questions to understand why I looked different. I love the beautiful spotted creatures I see on TV—Dalmatians, Great Danes, Appaloosa horses, cows, fish, and even caterpillars. I was not an animal; I was a human being, so maybe I looked strange and out of place, which could be why people could not stop looking at me.

I was about two years old when we moved to the town of New Brighton, Minnesota. As little children, my brothers and I would build forts in the living room, dragging in dining room chairs, end tables, and anything else we could move, to hold up the roof, made up of blankets or sheets. We would ride our stuffed animals down our stairs and then drag them into our new forts. Animal noises could be heard and an occasional "ouch" as a result from a playful punch from my oldest brother. We played there for hours, until Mom made us restore order to the space.

Shortly after the move, Mom was stressed out from the move and became sick. She was coughing, sneezing, sniffling and sitting on my brother Mike's bed who was also sick. With a damp washcloth in her hand, she gently put it on his forehead to comfort him. Even though it took a lot of effort for her to function, she was spooning soup into his mouth. I stood next to Mom with my hand on her lap hoping she could make my brother well. She told me to go to bed and everything would be all right. The next morning, I went into my brother's room and found Mom lying on the bed next to my brother as he slept peacefully. I looked at Mom's pretty face and she opened her eyes and smiled. Mom always loved, comforted and cared for us. She put our needs before hers, even when it meant discomfort for herself. Throughout Mom's life she always cared for others and never asked for anything in return, except love.

With Mom and Mike finally feeling better, we began to make the rounds to many physicians to figure out why I was spotted. I was about three years old when Mom took me to a class of student physicians in training hoping new technology and ambition would be able to figure it out. I had to sit on a tall stool in the middle of the cold classroom as I shook uncontrollably, wearing only my bottoms.

The instructor and students studied me up close and personal, taking note of my symptoms in order to come up with a diagnosis. Long, cold fingers poked at me, moving my arms and legs around, staring at me with frightening scowls. I was confused and not understanding why they were being so mean to me—and Mom was not stopping them. I kept my eyes on Mom, taking refuge in her face filled with worry, but she did not move towards me. Even though I felt terrified, I was glued to my seat, not sure what to do.

Once the inquisition was finally over, Mom lovingly picked me up and dressed me. We left and drove our van to a nearby store where Mom bought me a stuffed toy, a Dalmatian with spots just like mine. I quickly named him Jot. *I dearly loved that dog.* He comforted me in many ways that nothing and no one else could. He was soft and snuggly, and never once judged me. Jot loved me just the way I was. I took him to bed, outside and in the car, he was my constant companion. I loved him so much that I wanted a real live Jot, a dog that would be there for me but would also comfort me. Spots defined me, I thought, so if I had something by my side that was also spotted, I felt it would be like a secret society, and we would have each other to get through the hard times. But no matter how many tears I shed or how hard I pleaded, Mom never agreed to get me a real Dalmatian.

The doctors eventually diagnosed me with Urticaria Pigmentosa, a skin condition diagnosed in less than 200,000 people in the United States. It presents an ongoing allergic reaction, caused by the overreaction of mast cells, the immune cells that fight off infection. Symptoms include red spots that tend to itch badly when the body is overheated or the spots are scratched. There is no known cure for this condition. Nothing can be done to make the spots go away quickly. We were told they would slowly go away on their own throughout my childhood, and would be nearly gone by the time I was an adult. I still do have some spots, but they are very few in number and very light in color.
When I was a child, neighborhood mothers at the community swimming pool would pull their children to the other side of the pool and would not let them play with me. That did not stop me—not for a second. I loved the water and the way it would cool and soothe my itchy spots. I would leap into the water without fear and swim until I could swim no more. I was only about three years old and was too young to know that there were swim techniques like the crawl or the backstroke. I knew Mom would be at the other end of the pool to pluck me out of the water when I came to the surface.

As soon as I could write, I penned a song on a piece of paper called, "Please Don't Hurt My Little Girl." The lyrics were simple. "Please don't hurt my little girl, please don't hurt my little girl, please don't hurt my little girl." After we returned home from one of these outings where I could see people staring at me or pulling their children away, I would run up the stairs to the bathroom, close the door, and quietly sing my song. My young self was amazingly sweet and innocent, yet she was not always treated with love and acceptance.

My hope is the next time someone sees a little girl who is different, they will bend down on their knees, look her in the eyes, and sweetly have a conversation with her.

Even though I looked unusual, my childhood was "normal" in some regards. My favorite teacher was Mrs. Grant, my kindergarten teacher. She was beautiful with her long, blonde hair, pretty blue eyes, a heart of gold, and she treated me like a princess. Art class was another highlight, making many unique clay objects that I would bring home to Mom who'd usually place them in the center of our dining room table. When my hard work was acknowledged by placing it where everyone could see my efforts as an artist were appreciated, it gave me great joy. Acknowledgement for something I did well made me feel like I was okay after all, and not such an outsider with my unusual looks.

I was in kindergarten when I got my first boyfriend, Phillip. I liked him and visited his house, so that qualified him to be my boyfriend. He had beautiful thick, black, curly hair framing his cute round face. Just standing next to him felt special. It's fun to look back and remember the magical days of the first (play) date, first crush. I feel happy to think that even though I looked different, many people liked me regardless of how I looked.

But I did not have my first kiss with a boy until a few years later, under a bright star-filled sky on a hill overlooking the golf course near our home. A girl friend and I were on either side of this boy so there was no way for him to escape. I imagine he would have run away if he could have. We were in first or second grade and no one thought about my spots because we knew each other so well. We were not sure what a kiss really was, but my friend and I decided we should try it out on this boy, so we both kissed him. With a huge happy smile on my face, I looked at my friend, with my eyes twinkling like the stars above, and we did it. There was no second kiss, but at least I got that first one out of the way. He accepted me and was willing to put up with my giddy girl ways without a protest, and he didn't move his face away or say we were being silly.

In our neighborhood every house on our street except for one, had kids in it. With my high energy it was not hard to meet kids on our street. I was always outside running around, skipping, or climbing trees that had low limbs for me to grab on to. Susie, from the green house across the street and three houses down, was always outside because her mom liked the house clean and did not like noisy messy kids around. Susie was my constant companion. I had fun times with all the neighborhood friends who knew me and accepted my spots. We played games like ding-dong ditch, kick-the-can and had crab-apple fights. We made prank phone calls asking the person on the other end of the phone if their refrigerator was running, and then telling them they'd better go and catch it. All of our good-for-nothing tricks were innocent enough in nature, and we never got in trouble aside from a mean look here and there from our neighbor who did not have any kids.

But even though I had found a group of friends, I had not shaken off the feeling that other people made fun of me behind my back. I lashed out.

I was riding my bike up and down my street when I saw Stevie, who had a very large square head, in his driveway about seven doors down from me. "Hey TV head!" I yelled at him as I sped past. Now the spotted leopard was yelling bullying words at another kid. *If I hurt you first, you can't hurt me.* I did not do this often, but the couple times

I did, still hurt me deep down inside. He was the sweetest boy, and I saw the hurt on his face. No one ever reprimanded me for my outburst. I knew what it felt to be rejected so this was a rare incident in my life. If I could find him today, I would apologize.

Since I had three daring older brothers and I copied what they did, I was called a tomboy. I tried to keep up with them. If they climbed up the woodpile behind the house to get on the roof and jump off, I would too.

When I was in first grade my brothers enjoyed playing ice hockey; thus I followed suit. I would often take slap shots at goals on our asphalt driveway while wearing my brown, stitched, cowboy boots. On one particular day, I was pretending we were in an ice arena playing hockey with a girlfriend who was also a tomboy. I was gearing up for the best shot ever, bringing my hockey stick way back for the swing and stopped short only when my stick hit my friend's mouth and broke one of her front top teeth. *I wonder if she thinks of me when she looks in the mirror and sees her capped front tooth.* I felt horrible about hurting her, but at age six, I was also afraid she would not come back to play. She was my best friend and I would never dream of hurting her. We played together every day and often slept over at each other's house. I was so happy when she arrived back home from the dentist and ran to me smiling with her hockey stick in her hand.

I was hardly tall enough to see over the kitchen table, yet I could see Dad leaning back in his chair at the head of the table with his legs crossed and boots up on the table. My parents were discussing divorce, and how he was going to marry my friend's mom. That same year Mom married my friend's dad. Before this bizarre parent-swapping event, our two families were the best of friends.

After Mom's re-marriage, my stepdad brought his children to live with us. With my friends living in our house, we enjoyed playtime, all of the time. We didn't have to spend time traveling to each other's house, because we now lived in the same house.

Through all this time of turmoil, change and chaos, my brothers raced a minibike around our yard. What my brothers did, I wanted to do too. Unfortunately, my first experience on a motorbike did not go as planned. I was seven years old, and was given only basic instructions from my stepdad.

As I gave it gas, I ended up driving it straight into the nearest tree. But once I realized I was fine, with no broken bones, I got back on and learned how to use the brake pedal to stop. The thrill of doing something fun and challenging put me back on that seat even though I'd fallen off, because a little dirt and bruises have never kept me down.

After years of watching my brothers play hockey, I began to play Ringette in the fifth grade. Ringette is a game played on the ice, similar to hockey, except it has only the straight stick and not the curved blade at the bottom, and instead of a puck we used a soft ring that was open in the middle so the stick could be inserted in it to drag the ring around the ice and shoot on the goal. We wore protective helmets with mouth guards, which was a good thing because I played rough.

The rules of Ringette do not allow checking, which like in hockey meant aggressive body contact with the other team's members, but that did not stop me. Instead I spent a lot of time in the penalty box. I could not help it; it was my thing. I absolutely loved making goals, and reacted badly when someone got in my way. Skating fast, stealing the ring from other players, and bumping into them here and there was a great release for my energy and aggression. Back in those days girls did not play hockey, which was too bad because I think I could have become a famous woman hockey pro, if there was such a thing.

Thinking back on my Ringette days with aggressive skating and my need to check, it was probably a good way for me to release the intense frustration I had with life that was beyond my control. I could not stop people from being mean and staring so I took it out on the ice. I was lucky that my aggressiveness never hurt anyone.

I moved from the ice rink to the snowmobile, another one of my favorite cold-weather activities. After school I would run from the bus to the house to get bundled up in layers of warm clothes, helmets and gloves before heading out with my siblings to the snowmobiles. We had two of them, one for the girls and one for the boys. Since there were so many kids and only two sleds, we would take turns driving. When that became boring, we would lie on the ground, on our back, grab hold of the snowmobile rear seat handle while the driver dragged us all around creation. And while it was not the safest occupation, we were just kids who wanted to have fun.

One day, there were four of us out on the snowmobiles. I was driving one, with my stepsister Julie sitting behind me while my stepbrother, Sam drove the other one with my stepsister Katy riding with him. We were chasing each other all over the chain of lakes and through the woods near our home in Maplewood. Sam was flying behind us when Julie and I decided to race up and down some hills by Kohlman Lake.

We'd been snowmobiling for a while when I realized we'd lost track of Sam and Katy. So, after flying up a hill I decided to stop to see if I could spot them anywhere. After looking around, I saw them speeding over the hill and heading straight toward us. They were going so fast that Sam did not have time to swerve out of our way, and ended up smashing into us, side against side with Katy's leg caught between them when we collided. We quickly jumped off our snowmobiles and ran to see how she was doing.

Katy's face was twisted in pain as Sam and Julie did their best to care for her, I tried to be the entertainment to distract her. There I was playing the part of monkey girl covered from head to toe in my heavy winter gear, swinging from a nearby tree acting like a lunatic in an effort to make her laugh. It worked for a bit, and then she would get another stabbing pain, which meant her relief was short-lived. We decided to get her to a doctor so we carefully loaded her onto the snowmobile and sped home so Mom could drive her to the hospital. After X-rays, they discovered her leg was broken and she ended up wearing a huge, clunky cast for most of the remaining winter.

Winters in Minnesota can be a lot of fun when you're a kid. Skating on the lakes, sliding down hills, and whooshing across thick, powdery snow is easy when you're wearing those massive, funny-looking snowshoes. There's nothing better than cross-country skiing over all those flat trails through the woods or skiing down long hills overlooking the picturesque frozen lakes. As a child we routinely put on layer after layer of clothes and never minded the subzero temperatures and piercing, blowing snow.

When we were stuck at home, we got bored with snowball fights and invented a new game. "Betcha I can hit one first!" I would yell at my brothers as we stood on top of the high hill next to our house. We loaded ourselves up with snowballs, and were ready to fire one at the next passing car down below, feeling confident they could not see us. When we spotted headlights, we were ready. Fire! We all unleashed our fury on the unsuspecting car below. In the frenzy we are not sure who actually succeeded in hitting the car as snowballs were flying everywhere. This type of attack was played out many times until we noticed Mom standing behind us demanding to know what was going on. One of the drivers pulled around to the other side of our house, marched up the stairs and lodged their complaint about the snowball assault. The fun ended quickly, once Mom was on the scene.

Many times in my life I got lost in the fun and adventure with family and friends, and thought my spots had disappeared, even if it was just for a short while. I feel grateful for those days where I was rewarded with the momentary reprieves from the staring and anguish of my physical condition of being a spotted girl—and instead it was replaced with love and acceptance.

Chapter 3

Parent Swap

"When I was in the fourth grade, I was working hard on my multiplication tables, when someone suddenly called me 'pizza face.'"

Before this bizarre parent-swapping event, our two families had been the best of friends. Although this was a confusing time for me, I was happy that my friends now lived with me. It made for many fun times in our house. Rarely did we fight, and we continued to be friends after my new step-sisters moved in. Now we played with our Barbie dolls all day long instead of once in a while when we visited each other's house.

All three of us girls had banana-seat bikes with tassels coming out of the handle bars and baskets to hold our toys as we pedaled around our neighborhood all day long and played in our rooms for hours at night until it was time to go to bed. My stepsisters were identical twins, but I could tell them apart just by hearing their voice. From our kids' perspective, the divorce did not affect us other than Mom was very upset over it and was cranky a lot of the time.

Dad was like a happy, giddy kid again, living in an apartment with his girlfriend, Darcy, soon to be his wife. I was not invited to their wedding, so I have no memories about when and where they were married. It would have been fun to get a new fancy dress and be in their wedding. I remember wanting to throw flower petals down the center aisle for the wedding march. I did not live with them before or after they were married, nor did any of my siblings at first. I rarely saw him or his new wife except once or so a month.

Fairly soon after they were married, Dad's new wife Darcy decided she wanted to see her twin daughters that lived with me and the rest of the gang. When Darcy pulled into the driveway, Mom told all us girls to go out, get in the car, and have a great day. At the time I did not know I was not invited, which explained the unhappy look on Darcy's face when I cheerfully entered her car and sat down expecting a shopping day filled with fun. Later Mom told me that it was just supposed to be her twins.

At first Dad and his new wife refused to take responsibility for any of their combined eight children…maybe they did not want their honeymoon to end. But after a while they took the youngest child, Brett, who was just two. He was a quiet boy with blonde hair and eyes the color of a gentle drop of rain on a blue cornflower petal.

With Dad out of the picture most of the time, I became very close to my grandpa. He was a quiet man, simple and unpretentious, with thick gray hair and a gentle smile. He always wore a light blue button-up shirt, and dark blue cotton work pants. His shirts all had a pocket on the chest and in the pocket, he always carried a small notebook that he often consulted and frequently made notes.

His small, neat apartment was located between my house and our school so we made it a habit to stop and see him almost every day. I would run up to his first-floor picture window and frantically motion for him to go to the door and let us in. We spent many magical hours in his cozy studio apartment. He had lived an incredibly mesmerizing life, and I loved hearing all about it, as well as seeing evidence that he'd so diligently collected over the years.

He had jewelry boxes full of photos and a wide range of trinkets he had collected along the way. I called them his treasure boxes. For hours he would tell detailed stories of the origin of the precious mementos, explain where the photos were taken, and answer my endless questions. My favorite item, a single gold earring, had no history that he knew of. Over the years I often tried to imagine where it came from and why there was only one. *Did the person have only one ear, or maybe the earring was worn in their nose?* Today his treasure boxes are in my possession, and I have fond memories when I look at their contents.

Recently I was looking at a photo of Grandpa, my brothers and me, sitting on a brick fireplace ledge at our old house in New Brighton on 17th Avenue. My brother Todd is grinning ear to ear, while my brother Mike wears a serious look. Grandpa is looking to the side and not at the camera, and my brother Scott is sitting on Grandpa's left, also grinning a happy smile. The most compelling thing about the photo is that my hand is on Grandpa's leg as if to say: this is my grandpa, and I am thrilled to be sitting beside him. My grandpa replaced my dad because he was the one that loved, cared, listened to me, and never once did he let me down.

I have often wondered what my life would have been like if Dad had remained faithful to my mom. We probably would have stayed in the neighborhood where everyone accepted me and my spots. Had that happened, I think my life would have been much different than it is today, because I could have remained in my comfort zone instead of repeatedly stepping out to re-acclimate to each new situation. However, that also means I am far more independent than I would have been, and the many more experiences I have had, both good and bad, have shaped and molded me into a stronger, more resilient person than I might have been otherwise.

I did not learn about our new and larger family's upcoming move until it was already planned. My brother told me about it when we were in our backyard tree fort. I was furious.

"Why do we have to move?" I screamed, slamming the front door behind me as I entered the house.

"Our family is way too big for this house," Mom calmly replied. She did not even look up from the paper she was reading.

"Then let's make it bigger," I replied angrily. "Why can't we just add on to our house and make it bigger?"

"We've thought about ways to make it larger, but it's just too expensive." Mom finally looked up from her paper, with an understanding smile. "You're going to love the new house. It's on a lake. You love swimming."

I stamped my foot and turned my head away. "No one makes fun of me in this neighborhood. You know how it is when we go places where people don't know me. They stare. They don't want to get near me. They think I'm contagious."

The hardest part of the move was that I had to leave Grandpa behind, a man I dearly loved. I rarely saw Grandpa after we moved away from him. Not seeing him on a daily basis left an empty hole in my heart because he was my father figure, and we had a very close relationship.

After we moved, I was registered for second grade at the new elementary school. The school had a program for troubled kids and apparently I had been diagnosed as a troubled kid because I was placed in that program. I do not recall any special tests I took for this, so I always thought my previous school told them something to make this decision. They were probably glad they made this assumption since I do recall a fight or two that I was a part of on the school playground. The program had us outside most of the time running around in an attempt to use up our endless energy. I loved it outside and was happy not to be in the stuffy, boring classrooms. My most vivid memory of the program is of a boy who would put frogs on a log and then smash them with rocks. Like I said, it was a program for troubled kids....

As I grew older, the kids around me weren't so sweet and innocent anymore. When I was in the fourth grade, I was working hard on my multiplication tables, when someone suddenly called me "pizza face." After I heard those words my mind immediately started to think of myself in a new light. I looked ugly. I looked like a pizza. After the long bus ride home, safe in my room, I lay in bed and listened to the laughter from the kids playing outside through my open window. My spots were bright red, itchy and inflamed again, so no way was I going out there to play because they would notice them for sure. Instead I stayed in my room and tucked in the sheet all around the bed and put a fan at the far end so the air could cool my skin.

Later I told Mom what had happened in school and how I felt as a ten-year-old—that in order to be like the other kids and be accepted, I needed to conceal my difference. We talked about it and we decided to buy makeup. We drove to Target and looked at the endless makeup options. How do you cover pizza on your face? We looked at all of the color options. Foundation or concealer? Powder or liquid? We finally decided on both liquid foundation and a stick concealer, similar to a lipstick tube, in a shade matching my beige skin tone. I started wearing makeup to mask the spots on my face, and I made sure I always wore long pants and long sleeves to hide the spots on my extremities, even when outside on scorching-hot summer days. Playing softball where everyone else at school was wearing shorts and tank tops, I wore my terry cloth zip-up navy blue long sleeve sweatshirt with red trim and long jeans. I was hot and sweaty, but accepted by my classmates. I put up an emotional wall and learned to hide the spots so I could not be wounded again.

I learned how to look good on the outside so my peers would not tease me, but on the inside I still felt very spotted and ashamed of my looks. My hurt was covered up, pushed down to the lowest depths inside of me. I felt to be accepted I had to be someone else, someone that looked un-flawed.

With makeup, I no longer stood out from the crowd, I was surprised when new friends began popping up all over, and who soon grew accustomed to my new appearance. It was not long before I was living a "normal" life, being invited to sleepovers at the homes of my new friends. I would spend all night wearing makeup and long sleeved, full-length pajamas so no one could see my spots. My friends never saw the spots, and did not seem to think it was a big deal that I was covered from head to toe. We had lots of fun, sometimes staying up all night, discussing the cute guys at school or the latest softball game we won or lost.

Roller-skating at Saints North offered many chances to mix with guys my own age. We took part in what we called a "snowball" skate where we would stand in a circle, guys on one side, girls on the other, and we would skate back and forth and ask someone from the other side to roller dance with us. Oh, those couple's skate dances were the best. I was over-the-top with joy whenever I was asked to skate or someone responded yes when I asked. I have happy memories of those wonderful times. One night of skating and flirting with some boys, my friends and I were offered a ride home. I was excited because I felt accepted. I called Mom to tell her about it and ask if it was alright that I get a ride home from them. Mom, not agreeing with my enthusiasm, had a very different reaction to the invitation and said no. As it tends to do, life continued despite my big disappointment.

Our family vacations included taking two cars to hold everyone, plus the camping equipment, and we used walkie-talkies to talk between cars. John Denver songs were always blaring in our car as we sang, "Country roads, take me home…" Those vacations were a lot of fun, as well as some excitement. One trip to Colorado when I was around 12 was an especially memorable experience that we still talk about.

We hiked and played in the stream near our campsite, but we were not allowed to go far. A couple of my brothers, one and six years older than I was, thought it would be fun to hike up the mountain by themselves. I am not sure whether that hike was parent-sanctioned or not, but they took off alone. As the day was winding down, they still had not returned from the mountain, and our parents began to worry. Once the sun had set, they notified the park ranger that the boys were still up there, all alone. I became very excited as I watched the helicopter searchlight scour the area. Within hours, they rescued my brothers from their perch on the mountain and were returned to us, safe and sound. From what the boys said, they made the climb upward without any problems, but the rocks kept sliding out from under their feet when they attempted to descend. Afraid of falling, they chose to stay put and wait for someone to come and get them.

The following year our family took a trip to Northern Minnesota along Lake Superior. We drove a few hours north and arrived at the campground, unloaded the vehicles, set up the tents and prepared for a fun day of adventure. After exploring the small waterfall and river near our camp, we hiked west along the river. In good spirits after a full day of hiking, back at camp, we dared each other to swim in freezing cold Lake Superior. After winding down the day with a campfire meal, we got our sleeping bags situated before heading to bed. The stars were bright and beautiful without competition from the city lights. We had multiple tents to fit our family of nine. The girls had their own tent, parents in one tent and the four boys would split up into two small tents. In our girls' tent I would use little white towelettes to remove my makeup before my head hit the pillow.

Early in the morning, before my sisters would start to wake, as the birds would begin to sing and the sun just starting to peek over the horizon, I would look into the side mirror of our big brown car, pull out my makeup and cover my spots to be ready to face the day. My "wall" was always up, and I felt the need to conceal my spots everywhere. Family, friends, or strangers needed to see a spotless face—or so I thought.

After we returned home from that trip, my parents decided it would be a good idea to turn our home into an emergency shelter for foster kids that were taken out of a bad situation and had nowhere to live. No doubt, there's a great need for this service and I support it. I was in my early teens at the time, and it's a bit tricky to have kids removed from emergency situations and dropped off at your home at all hours of the day and night. In our case it made for some very short nights, because teenagers were frequently in need of emergency placements. We took in only a few boys at a time because each foster boy would room with one of my brothers. For this, my parents earned a small monthly stipend for their care.

Some of the boys were very young and scared. Mom did a great job with the kids, and I know they greatly appreciated our home while they waited for a more permanent situation. I remember having a conversation in our kitchen with one of the scared young boys as he told me his story and how much it meant to him being able to come to our home where we were all nice to him. Most boys stayed with us just a short time because we were an emergency shelter home and not a foster home. Once in a while when there was nowhere for a kid to be placed, he would stay with us for many months, and when those kids left, we always felt like we were doing the right thing, otherwise where would they have lived—on the streets?

One incident occurred at the beach by our house that made me fearful of having the boys in our home. One of the older boys and I had gone for a walk down the road by the lake, and then he suggested we go to our beach, which is down a steep hill and very secluded. I thought nothing of it until we sat on the picnic table chatting and the conversation turned to one of a sexual nature. My 12-year-old body went into high alert and told me I better get out of there fast before something happened. I quickly ran up the beach stairs, up the hill to our house and into the safety of my bedroom. After that, I kept my distance from the older boys as much as possible.

Many of the shelter boys in our house educated us in ways you usually do not learn at your local school. I recall we had houseplants arranged on a wide ledge along one wall in our family room, some of which were rich green cannabis plants, though we were certainly unaware of it at the time. Because we were an emergency shelter home, the police were always coming or going, dropping off or picking up the latest emergency placement, but for some reason they never noticed the plants. Our foster kids were street smart and excited to share that knowledge with us kids. I have no idea who planted them or brought them home. All I know is shortly after that, the plants magically disappeared one day and never returned to their perch on the ledge.

While the foster boys were sometimes a negative influence on my brothers, Tim terrified Mom. He lived with us for a few years before Mom felt that at the age of 19, he needed to move out and be responsible for himself. One night in particular I remember Mom pacing back and forth looking frightened. With all the lights off in the house, we looked outside to see if Tim was out there. She was convinced it had become his life's mission to kill her. Thankfully, he never succeeded in doing that.

Apparently Tim thought the next best thing was to burn down our detached garage. I was visiting Grandpa's home when I received a call telling me our garage burned down. I was stunned and couldn't imagine it. When I returned home and saw a large black charred heap where our garage use to stand, I stood motionless and looked at the smoldering embers with eyes threatening tears.

In the end, Tim was caught, convicted and served time for his crime. After the fire, it was strange to see the melted items like Scott's sailboat in the burned-out shell of a garage. Luckily our insurance covered the damage and most of the lost items. Our garage was re-built and the items were replaced. Shortly after we had our new garage and the items were replaced, we were re-arranging its contents, when someone had the nerve to sneak in and steal our new bikes right out from under our noses.

At the time I could not understand what the foster kids went through who didn't have a safe home to live in—and needed to be sheltered at our house. I was too young to comprehend what their life was like before they came to us. Some were confused, abused, lonely, and rejected, and some of them lashed out because they were experiencing hard-to-understand life experiences and losses. Looking back I am glad we helped these boys because overall a lot of good came out of it. When the boys arrived at our house they were typically scared and withdrawn. When they left our home, they usually had a different attitude because they had received kindness, safe living quarters and hot meals from us. To the average person these things may be taken for granted, but for these boys that were either living in a horrible situation or on the streets, it was usually appreciated. *Giving hope to those boys made it all worth it.*

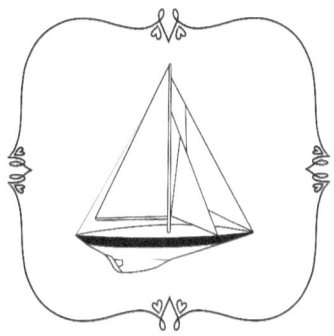

Chapter 4

Scott Goes to Heaven

"Another of his loves was a sailboat he acquired at an auction that was long past its prime, decrepit, something that would ultimately require an enormous amount of time and energy to bring it back to life."

The last conversation I had with my brother Scott was while he was getting some food and I was in the adjoining room watching TV.

"Hey Scott, whatcha up to on this crazy rainy day?"

"Going to kick around at the Minnesota State Fair with my buddy."

"You're crazy, it's pouring cats and dogs out there!" I said, with a laugh.

"Yeah, I know, but it will quit later, so we're headed out anyways."

"If you're set on going, at least grab a bunch of fresh brownies I just baked. They are sitting on the kitchen counter."

He died later that day on August 28, 1979, at age sixteen.

As Scott was driving east on County Road D to Highway 61 it was still pouring a blinding, deluge of rain. He stopped before turning onto the highway, but because it was raining so hard, and the approaching vehicle did not have its lights on, my brother never saw the truck that hit and killed him.

When a friend called to tell us that Scott was in a car accident, I frantically tried to phone the hospital to get more information. The nurse who answered the phone would only tell me that my mom was on her way home from the hospital, and I would have to wait and talk to her.

My bedroom overlooked the steep staircase that led up the hill from the garage, and I stood glued to the window in anticipation of her arrival. Finally, I saw her slowly walking up the stairs, and seeing her downcast face, I instantly knew my brother was gone. I ran downstairs, flew out the back door, grabbed Mom and we held tightly to each other, sobbing a river of tears until there were no tears left in us.

Todd, my oldest brother, wanted to go to the mortuary with Grandpa to confirm it was Scott. I wanted to be with Scott forever so I took off my sterling silver necklace that had a cross and heart embossed on a solid round circle and handed it to Todd.

"Please make sure the mortician puts this around Scott's neck so I can always be with him," I said choking back tears.

The day of the funeral we all quietly put on our nicest clothes and drove to our church in St. Paul. We were first to arrive so we could say our private good-byes to Scott. Sitting in the sanctuary pew, looking at the casket in front, I could not stop my eyes from dripping a steady stream of tears. I have no idea what was said during the funeral because I heard none of it. When the men walked over, took hold of the handles on the casket and slowly wheeled it down the aisle, we stood up and followed behind Scott. As I was walking down the aisle, the only thing I remember noticing was the entire church was full of people, with not one single spot open.

After we buried Scott, close friends and family came to our house to give us their condolences and reminisce. We sat on the grass in our backyard overlooking the lake with a box of photos. Pulling each photo out, looking at it and talking about what we had done that day with Scott brought him back to life for us, in that moment.

When the last guest left, Mom closed herself off from the world in her bedroom and went into a deep depression.

Knocking on the door I asked, "Mom, can I go to the mall with Debbie?"

From behind the door that rarely opened anymore, she responded, "Sure, do whatever you want."

Days became weeks that felt like years before Mom could laugh again.

Scott died at the end of summer of 1979, and I had to start school just a short while later. My friends were very helpful in comforting me while I tried to live a life without my close friend, Scott. Today I have a blue envelope with mementoes from that terrible time in my life. I have the funeral bulletin and notes from friends that I have re-read over the years. My friends were a blessing to me as I tried to create a life without Scott. Tammy, one of my close friends wrote me a note, gave it to me in school and asked me to read it when I got home. I still have this note and it begins with "I am real sorry to have heard about your brother" and ends with "friends, forever and ever."

A couple of months after his death, one of Scott's friends called with a question. "Scott loaned me many of his records, and I still have them. What do you want me to do with them?" I paused, thought about it, asked Mom and then told him to keep the records. Scott loved music and was happy to share his joy with others. He even made two large wooden speakers in shop class so he could crank up the music loud and rock the house. I now look at those classic speakers and feel like he is still with me. His hands crafted every piece of wood and accessories on those speakers. Surely, part of him remains within them.

Another of his loves was a sailboat he acquired at an auction that was long past its prime, decrepit, something that would ultimately require an enormous amount of time and energy to bring it back to life. He took a great deal of pride in fixing up that boat. Many days he would be in the backyard with the boat stretched across two wooden stands, working into the late hours of the night to refinish the surface and make her look beautiful again. That same summer he decided to try something else new, sewing a winter ski jacket that was blue on the outside with bright, sunny yellow fabric lining on the inside. With a family the size of ours, Mom was always sewing on some project or another, so Scott decided he could do it too. I was amazed when I saw the beautiful finished jacket, but it was a "one and done," and I never saw him sew anything again.

Scott was very smart and because I followed him by a couple of years in school, all of my teachers had high expectations for me. "I'm sure you're going to be the top of the class just like Scott was," all of my teachers would say when they first met me and heard my last name.

But later on, when I began to receive A's, B's and an occasional C, teachers would say, "Why aren't you getting straight A's like Scott?" I would shrug. What was there to say? I am not Scott, I would say dejectedly to myself. *Scott was a genius and I am not.*

Trying to live up to Scott's reputation was difficult because I hated sitting still in class and listening to a teacher, so many times my grades would suffer. Trying to improve my grades, I cheated on my math homework once. I took my homework home to work on it, but my dog peed on it so I had to tell my teacher I needed the homework again. I used a calculator to do the multiplication work and turned it in the next day, telling him I did not want to spend time rewriting the multiplication work I had done the first time so I just jotted down the answers. I did not get caught, so I tried it again, but the next time, I cheated in a very different way.

This time it was spelling, and I wrote the words down and covered it with a clean sheet of paper so you could faintly see them through the paper. Apparently, that was not a new or unique way of cheating, because I was busted and received a big fat "F" for the spelling test. I imagine teachers could write volumes on the number of ways students cheat on tests.

Scott and I had competed in everything because we were the closest in age and size. Even though I loved Scott, my jealousy of his intelligence pushed me on to always compete with him.

"I am bigger than you are!" I once teased Scott heartily.

"Am not, I am way bigger than you are!" Scott countered with a big grin.

"Let's get on the scale to prove it, smarty pants!" I said, full of confidence. We laughed heartily when the scale said we both weighed 128 pounds.

The Hobbit and *Watership Down* were at the top of Scott's favorite book list. I also loved reading books, and we often exchanged books. Scott made me laugh when he sat in the recliner with the lower half of his body on the chair and the upper half of his body on the floor, eyes glued to the pages of his latest book.

In the summer of 1979 when Scott was sixteen, he was just beginning to come into his own and become a young man. YMCA Camp Widjiwagan made a big impact on his life and was instrumental in building his courage as a leader. At camp he made a number of good friends, went on unforgettable wilderness adventures, learned leadership skills, and built up his confidence. I have a photo taken at that time where I can see his smiling face as he stands next to a canoe at Camp Widjiwagan. It's the last photo taken of him, but it comforts me knowing he was happy.

Because of the incredibly sad memories of Scott that remained in that house, the neighborhood and the nearby location where he died, it was not long before we packed up and moved to Ohio. Memories of that move include watching our cat pant in the un-air-conditioned, pastel blue, Oldsmobile Delta 88. Because of the extreme heat and humidity, she was uncomfortable and until that trip I'd never seen a cat panting.

I understood the reason for the move, but I still was not happy about it, because I would once again have to make all new friends who would be unfamiliar with my spots. I was leaving behind my friend Debbie. We told each other everything, which usually included what guy was our latest crush. We bought rings that were the same and called them our forever friendship rings. We wrote notes to each other during school and handed them off as we passed in the hallway. Leaving her was hard.

When I lived in Maplewood before we moved to Ohio, Grandpa and I would go on antique hunts every couple of months. I was always in search of beautiful old jewelry pieces, and he loved clocks. We would walk around Apache Plaza or another mall and look at every table in the hopes of finding a cheap but amazing piece of history. I did not have much money so I would pick up a piece of jewelry, look at the price tag and then look at Grandpa to see his reaction to the price. He usually bought me one item each time we went on our outings.

While living in Maplewood as a young teenager, Grandpa taught me to drive when we took road trips to visit Mom's sister Ruth and my cousins in Guthrie Center, Iowa. I did not get to see Grandpa very often after the move so I loved our rare and memorable vacations together. They were week-long trips during our school's summer break. It was our special adventure, just the two of us. Before we left, we would make bologna and cheese sandwiches to eat on the way, wrap them in plastic wrap and tuck them in a box with other supplies for the trip. As we drove, the sun would shine in the car windows and warm our sandwiches; even now I can still taste that yummy melted cheese, a memory that remains vivid forty years later.

The first time Grandpa let me drive was on a country highway, and when a semi-truck passed me, the car shook and I was scared, but not enough to say anything because I did not want to stop driving. At my cousins' farm, they had many acres of corn, and they had a road that went through the cornfield to our other cousin's house. A red Volkswagen

Bug was called the kid's car, and we could drive back and forth on this cornfield road anytime we wanted. Yep, I just about wore the tires off that poor old car when I visited their house in Iowa. This newfound freedom of driving was a thrill for me, and I never wanted it to end. Of course it did end, but I looked forward to any chance I could drive again.

It was a red-letter day when I earned my driver's license. Since I'd been driving for several years before I took the driver's education test, I passed with flying colors. Once I got home with my new license in hand, I took our family's red Toyota Celica and drove as fast as I could, going back and forth on the remote country roads near our home in Hamilton, Ohio. I'd never before felt so free. I did not think about the fact that it was not safe. I could have hit a cow, a dog, a cat, or even a human being. I just cherished the freedom, and to this day look for any excuse to take a road trip.

My first day at my new school in Ohio I met a girl named Tara in my Biology class. The room smelled bad and had cockroaches running around. I remember watching a cockroach climb up inside a boy's pant leg. I did not know what to do. Do you interrupt the class and say, "Hey there is a cockroach going up your pants"? I chose to keep my mouth shut, and he never moved his leg or said anything so I guess the cockroach did not find anything interesting in there and left on the other side where I could not see it.

Tara and I were friends the entire time I lived in Ohio. Since she was my first friend on my first day of school, I felt thankful I did not have to sit alone at lunch. After school we would take long walks in the small downtown area of Hamilton and talked about our latest boyfriends or what our family was up to. Neither of us had much money so we stayed outside where it was free.

Rachel was another friend of mine from school, and we did almost everything together. Each school day I would pick her up in my red Toyota Celica and drive her to school so we could have fun before school. She was about a foot shorter than I was, so it was funny to walk down the hall together because we looked mismatched with the size difference. Our friendship lasted after we graduated from high school. We were even in each other's weddings, and though neither marriage lasted, our friendship stayed strong while I lived in Ohio. After I moved back to Minnesota, I would fly to Ohio about once a year to visit Rachel.

One night while I was in high school, I picked up a girlfriend for a night out and noticed that she wore makeup not only on her face but also on her neck, which is what I always did to cover my spots. I was really surprised that she imitated my behavior. I felt flattered that she thought what I was doing looked good enough that she wanted to do it too.

When I went to prom, I was able to enjoy spending time with my friends. I did what I had to do to fit in. Covering my spots for many years had become a habitual part of my routine. Spot covering actually takes a bit of time, and I always felt like I was an artist creating a painting. I would start off with concealer and cover the spots. Next I would go over those with foundation and then a light dusting of powder to set my creation. After a few years of doing this, I added in eye shadow, blush and mascara. While most women probably only wear one pair of pantyhose, I often wore two or three pairs at a time, depending on the length of my dress and how bright my spots were at the time.

My face full of makeup became my normal. If I did not wear my makeup, my family would question if I felt okay. I can count on my hands how many days a year I went without makeup back then and even now. I have become accustomed to my artistically made-up face, and feel that it has become part of my identity and feel strange without it.

Makeup is surprisingly very waterproof. I loved swimming so much that I was eager to be part of the high school swim team even though it took a great deal of courage. I called the head swimming coach before joining the team to get a sense of what the team was like. He assured me of the team's commitment of supporting each other, and how they were very friendly and welcoming to all newcomers. I agreed to join and was happy to find out the team was true to his words.

From the locker room to the pool I always wore a towel tightly wrapped around my body for warmth, and in an attempt to hide some of my spots. When I was in the water I could not see or hear what others had to say, so it did not bother me one way or the other. After the season was over and we had a banquet, I was awarded "most-improved swimmer."

In my senior year of high school, I quit the team so I could work at the same restaurant where my older brother Mike worked. He was now the closest to my age with Scott gone. At my new job I earned some extra spending money, hung out with Mike, and made new friends. I enjoyed making tacos, burritos, and pizzas. I liked break time the best when I could create my own food masterpieces and purchase them with my employee discount. However, I did not like it enough to want to do it full time forever.

Life was moving forward without Scott in our daily lives. There wasn't really any other choice. I learned to cope without him, thought about him often and talked about our adventures when he was still alive. I am thankful for the time we did have together. There are many great memories to hold me over until I see him again.

Chapter 5

Marriage

> *"Through Jim's endless love and patience with me,
> I slowly began to let my wall down and let
> him glimpse my personal struggles."*

Our little red house was quiet with my daughter upstairs taking a nap in the remodeled attic, and I was in the kitchen deciding what to have for dinner when I heard the phone ring.

"Hello," I casually answered.

I heard a male voice that I did not recognize say, "You don't know me, but I just thought you should be told—your husband is having an affair with Shelly here at work. I don't think it's right, so that's why I am calling to tell you," he said in a hurried voice and hung up.

My mind was spinning, not sure what to say, so I slowly hung up the phone.

My first marriage was doomed because of things that we both did and said—and I regret them. Along the way we both found comfort with people outside of our marriage, and we headed down a dangerous road. When we married, we were immature and had very little in the way of wisdom. I wonder if we would have married if I hadn't gotten pregnant. Being naïve, inexperienced parents, living without enough money to pay our bills, changed us both.

It's difficult to write about my own infidelity. My bad-girl years are a time I am not proud of and would prefer to leave out of this book, but then it would be incomplete.

Once Lisa became a toddler, I felt like my life was finally becoming manageable—and thankfully my depression had started to lift. I was lonely and started to do what my husband was doing…partying. It started off innocently enough, but because of my low self-esteem, when a guy who was very attractive, like a male model, came up and flirted with me, I ate up the attention and unfortunately that evening ended in a one-night stand.

When I went out with my single girlfriends, I did not plan on being an adulteress. But it was hard to resist when my husband was not around, and I was getting lots of attention from guys at the bars. Looking back in time, I wished I would have done things differently. I now feel the bar setting is not a good place for a lonely, married woman to be hanging out.

My sins haunted me for thirty years, making me feel like I was not worthy of God's love. It took me a long time to regain that sense of worth.

As an adult, my Mom and I loved giving each other advice. We both felt we had the answers to the world's problems, and were not afraid of telling everyone about it. When we had our talks, they were at Mom's kitchen table. On one such day as we discussed life, Mom had some "words of wisdom" she preached at me. "It's not like you have a lot of guys knocking on your door, so you should get married again as soon as you can find someone willing to tie the knot."

I knew she loved me and had my best interests in mind, so that's exactly what I did after my first marriage ended in divorce. I found someone to marry me. It's clear my next marriage definitely should never have happened. He was 29, lived with his parents, smoked pot and drank whiskey and beer every day. But he said he wanted to marry me, so in my mind at the time that was all that mattered.

Looking back on my early marriages, the best thing that came out of them were my beautiful daughters, though I would have done many things differently. Drinking and hanging out in bars only caused heartache when alcohol was involved. If I could change the past, I would have found Christian friends that would have encouraged me to attend bible studies instead of hanging out in bars. Our community of friends is important, and who we spend time with defines us, so we need to be selective. *Too bad I learned this late in life.*

Putting partying behind me, I started attending women's events at our church. "Women on the Edge" was my favorite group because we went dogsledding, snowshoeing, hiking, sailing, and other outdoor activities together. These events always included time in God's word and encouraging each other. I also attended a spiritual healing retreat that was very memorable. During this retreat we washed each other's feet as Jesus did, teaching us humility and service towards each other. I met Mary at this retreat. She had many health issues, and we all laid hands on her and prayed for her. After that event, Mary and I became friends.

Mary and I were both single and spent many memorable times together. We went to a Destiny's Child concert in downtown Minneapolis, traveled to a variety of restaurants, and attended church together. During this same time at a nearby bar an event happened that would change my life forever.

It was 2001, Jim Jackson was at a bar, and met a man named Virgil and the two began to talk. Virgil told Jim that he should meet his girlfriend so he called her over. Jim looked at Virgil's girlfriend and said, "Oh my gosh, it's Val! How are you?" As it turned out Val was one of the women he'd previously coached in softball. Val introduced Jim to her friend Mary, and they had a great evening reminiscing about old times.

This is the same Mary I met at a women's ministries healing retreat, and began spending time together. For her birthday she thought it would be fun to invite a bunch of friends to get together for drinks. Jim and I were both invited to attend.

When I first met Jim at that party, it was a heart-stopping moment. You see, I have always been drawn to well-developed muscles, and those that were visible through his tank top were indeed impressive. It was not long before we were chatting, flirting, and getting to know each other better, and before the night was over, he asked me out. I did not answer immediately because I was dating someone else at the time, and I did not think it would be fair to him, though I did not actually want to turn down Jim's invitation. When we were ready to leave, he walked me to my car and we said cordial good-byes.

A month later Mary and I were hanging out at a church's fall festival, enjoying the music when Mary asked if I thought we should call Jim to ask if he'd like to come and spend some time with us. Without a doubt, I was in favor of seeing him again so she phoned him, and he agreed to join us.

Jim arrived looking quite handsome in dark dress pants, a fleece pullover, dress shoes, and no socks. (He later admitted, he didn't have any clean socks). For a while we just hung out, and then someone suggested we play pool at a nearby bar. By the end of the night Jim and I were talking outside at his truck and once again he asked me out.

"Why would you want to go out with me? I've been divorced three times and have two kids," I said bluntly with my low self-esteem being too obvious.

"I'm not asking you to marry me, just to go out with me," Jim kindly reassured me.

Even though I had a smile on my face, I was a master of stuffing down my pain, suffering and insecurities. I could not fathom a strong handsome man like Jim wanting to go out with me, yet I desperately wanted to feel loved and accepted. Luckily for me he thought I was worthy.

For our first date we went to his son's football game. From then on, we started seeing each other on a daily basis, and alcohol was very available wherever we went. It appeared that he was trying to encourage me to drink alcohol so he could drink even more. One night we had dinner at a great steakhouse in downtown Minneapolis, and I watched as he repeatedly ordered more wine. By that time, we'd already had far too much to drink and were definitely drunk, in no condition to drive or do anything else. It did not take a brain surgeon to realize that his drinking was out of control.

Later that week, I went to visit Jim at his house. When I entered, he was taken by surprise.

"Jim, what did you put under the bathroom sink as I walked in?"

"Nothing," Jim replied sheepishly.

I walked to the bathroom, opened the cupboard under the sink and grabbed the bottle he stuffed under it.

"Is this bottle of Southern Comfort your nothing?" I asked, already knowing the answer.

The last straw occurred when Jim overturned his snowmobile with his son on it, and then later crashing into the back of mine. I was very upset that he could have injured his son, and felt I needed to break it off with him—I just could not date a roaring alcoholic. I was now in my mid 30's, learned from my past mistakes and had no intention of being with someone again that abused alcohol.

At that point, he realized he needed to get sober but did not know how. Though I was unaware of it at the time, he asked a dear friend to help him get into Hazelden Treatment Center's 28-day program, so he could kick the habit. About two weeks into the program he called to tell me he was there. He said he was really sorry for what he put me through. We talked every day on the phone for a week before I decided to visit him. If he was sincerely ready to get sober, I was willing to give him another chance. We got to know each other all over again. When he left Hazelden at the completion of his program, he moved in with me, and we have been together ever since. He's now been sober for 17 years.

When we first met, Jim was recently divorced too, and was also going through a court battle with a former business partner. I enjoy a challenge and Jim was definitely worth fighting for. I stayed by his side during the court battle and God blessed us, allowing us to win that battle as well. We're very grateful to God who put us together as soul mates.

Jim stated in the beginning he wasn't asking me to marry him, just asking for a date. And true to his words he never did ask me to marry him, I asked him to marry me, and he said yes. He loves to tell everyone that *I asked him!*

Through Jim's endless love and patience with me, I slowly began to let my wall down and let him glimpse my personal struggles. *I finally felt like I do deserve love and acceptance.* The spots that had felt like permanent marks—even after they were barely visible—did not control me anymore.

When I was younger I was looking for love and acceptance in the wrong places. I thought I should jump anytime a guy acted like he liked me and was not selective on who I should marry. I also was a convenient Christian so I did not truly understand that God's love was the number one love I needed. Once filled with God's love, you can take your time to find the human partner God has created for you.

I finally figured out that we are all deserving of glorious love. I learned not to settle for less than God's best. I am grateful to have found the love of my life, my soul mate. He was worth the wait.

Chapter 6

Motherhood

"As I looked up at it, the poem gave me a sense of comfort knowing that Jesus was beside me and would carry me through whatever was causing this nausea."

The *Footprints in the Sand* poem hung in my bathroom when I was a teenager in Ohio. But the first time I had really noticed the poem I was seventeen, had just eaten breakfast, felt nauseated and vomited. Thinking about what could be going on with my body, I realized I had missed my period. As I looked up at the poem, it gave me a sense of comfort knowing that God was beside me and would carry me through.

After school that day I drove to my boyfriend's house, told him I missed my period and I may be pregnant. He ran his hands through his thick, wavy brown hair and had a serious look.

"I could be wrong, maybe I just have the flu," I said, my voice shaky.

"Well, I guess we better go to a doctor and find out for sure," he said.

We went to a clinic in a nearby city to find out if I was pregnant. It did not take long to get the results: I was pregnant. Stepping out into the sunshine and walking along the sidewalk we thoughtfully discussed our options. After mulling over various ideas, we decided to get married and have the baby.

I put my hand on my belly and thought to myself, could there be life in there? I was not scared, because I knew I would love it no matter what. Yes, I was young, but I would be graduating from high school soon and then I would start my life as a mother and wife. Family was always very important to me, especially after losing my brother.

Finally, after a life filled with my physical spots and rejection from some people, my life might be full of happiness, acceptance and maybe even significance as a mother and wife. I began to look forward to becoming a mom to the baby growing in my belly—and looking forward to having a man love and accept me.

We planned for a traditional wedding two months before my due date at our church where we had met. Flowers were a must in my mind as they brought beauty to any occasion with their color and fragrance. To document this big day I wanted photos. This was the beginning of my new life, and I wanted to remember it always. My belly wasn't very big so I wanted the dress to be white because I wanted everyone to think I was a virgin. We found a gorgeous beaded high-waisted dress with long lace sleeves to cover my lingering spots that had not faded yet.

Music brings joy, yet our money was getting low so we decided to have family and friends provide the music. Our venue would be simple yet spacious in my parents' large walkout basement which had a vintage piano that was tuned for the occasion.

With my sugar addiction in full bloom, I visited many bakeries to taste test their cakes. It was hard to decide so I had to do a second taste testing to be sure I would make the right choice. I finally decided on a beautiful three-tiered cake with each tier having a different flavor: raspberry, chocolate and vanilla.

We were broke kids with no money so our honeymoon was spent in our small rented one-bedroom apartment on Ross Avenue in Hamilton, Ohio. The day after the wedding our family brought over all of the wedding gifts, and we were overjoyed with so much expression of love through gifts. Our small apartment was filled with people, laughter and lots of joy.

Because of my tall frame and lots of room for a baby, it was not very obvious I was pregnant so we kept it a secret until after the wedding. The shame did not sting as much with a ring on my finger when I told everyone that I was pregnant. I did not have to wait long to meet my baby. While at work making tacos and tending to the customers' orders, I suddenly felt like I had peed my pants. I quickly told my boss I had to go to the bathroom and ran downstairs to the basement bathroom. I pulled down my pants and could tell my water broke, and I had not peed in my pants. My due date was supposed to be in two weeks, but I kept calm. I knew that was not too early, so I focused on feeling happy that I would soon get to meet my baby that had been kicking me for months. I told my boss I had to go home, and then head to the hospital.

My home was only one block from work so I quickly walked home, and because it was Sunday evening, my husband was home. We packed up what I would need for the hospital stay and drove the couple miles to our town's hospital. I was excited for the birth of our child, and being naïve, thought it would be over in no time, little did I know…

After eighteen hours of excruciating pain, the nurse determined she needed to do something to help.

"You want to give me an enema and stick what where?!" disgusted, I shrieked at the nurse.

"You are not dilating and we need to get things going," she said firmly.

"That sure will get things going all right, in a nasty hurry!" I cried, my face twisted in pain.

Mom was always there for me, and even emptied my bedpan, which I think has to be one of the worst jobs ever.

After I gave birth, our pastor came to the hospital to pray with us. It was an especially sweet moment when we held our baby daughter's hands and prayed for her health and happiness.

I was released from the hospital after a couple of days, but my precious baby Lisa had jaundice. I was forced to leave her at the hospital for several extra days until her bilirubin level was within normal range. Since I was breastfeeding every few hours, I would drive back and forth to the hospital to feed her. I loved the closeness I had with her there, feeding her in the nursery, holding her eye to eye, skin to skin, and heart to heart. She was and is such a beautiful soul inside and out. I am thrilled to have given birth to her even though at the time, I thought it might kill me.

From the moment we got home, she simply would not stop crying, and I was exhausted. Fully depressed, I thought I would go crazy. I stayed in my pajamas for days, not wanting to dirty more clothes that I would have to wash. It took all of my energy to care for Lisa, and just when I finally was able to lie down, she would begin crying, for reasons unknown to me, and it would start all over again.

I was alone most all the time because my husband attended school, went to work—but he also partied in what little spare time he had left. Exhausted, yet needing to take care of my newborn baby, clean the house, do the extra laundry of dirty cloth diapers, buy the groceries and cook, it was all hard to do without any help. I survived on my own, with my baby—but our marriage did not make it more than about seven years.

Those were difficult days; I often wonder how I coped. It was the greatest challenge I'd ever had to face up to that point, and there was no training manual to consult or mentor to show me the way. It taught me something I might not have learned any other way; *sometimes we have to walk through very challenging, difficult times to learn a lesson that will be valuable as we move on.*

But if life was always easy, I wonder, would I really appreciate it or would I take it for granted? The hard times have made me a more thankful person because of what I have endured. I survived, with help. Looking back, the footprints poem was a true representation of how God led me and carried me through the dark times.

After a short stint in retail sales, I applied for and was hired to work full time as a Quality Inspector. I needed daycare for three-year-old Lisa. My boss told me about a daycare that she loved and highly recommended. When I scheduled a tour, I was surprised to find out they were renting two of the classrooms in my old elementary school. They also had access to the downstairs lunchroom they used for a gymnasium, and they also conducted evening parenting classes there.

It felt strange walking around in my old school, but decided it was the best place for my daughter. I felt like a single parent because my husband was never home, and I wanted to improve my parenting skills so I attended the classes. Lisa would have dinner and play with the kids upstairs while the parents had class downstairs. My parenting skills dramatically improved once I started attending their evening classes. I am very thankful for all that I learned those nights. With the knowledge on how to take care of and nurture my daughter, my life became less stressful and easier.

One suggestion that still stands out from that time was that if you have a child that won't stay in their room at night, you could put a lock on their door. Lock it when they were going to sleep, and then unlocking it when all was quiet. I never had this problem, but the school owners said they used that technique on their twin girls and it worked great. Years later, I was surprised when my daughter Lisa told me she decided to put a lock on her youngest daughter's door at night because she would not stay in her room. I did not tell her about this class, but that advice rose in my memory when she talked about her strategy. It just goes to show that everyone has a different idea on what parenting should look like, which is a good thing. We are all very unique and have different needs and wants.

Ten years later, after a divorce and remarriage I was pregnant again. In comparison, the birth of my second child was rather ordinary. This time, what you often hear was true: I forgot the pain after giving birth. When I went into labor early Wednesday morning. My second child did not take as long as the first one to deliver. I easily gave birth to Lacey, and by Sunday I was back at church teaching Sunday school.

But, once again, my new baby girl also struggled with some health issues early on. She had jaundice as well, but I was allowed to take her home this time, give fluids to dilute her bilirubin level and keep her in the sunlight as much as possible.

The day Lacey was released from the hospital we went to Lisa's school where she was in a class program with other students on the elementary gymnasium stage. I was surprised how much easier and more enjoyable it was to be a mother once I was older and far more mature. At age 29 I was much more capable of handling the 24/7 demands of a dependent young infant. I thanked God that He gave me another chance at motherhood after my harrowing teenage experience. I felt much more prepared this time around.

Unfortunately, I felt the need to divorce Lacey's dad. His daily use of alcohol and smoking was not slowing down. He would go over to his friend's house, get drunk and then drive home. As Lisa was getting older, she and her stepdad did not get along. The last straw came when he grabbed Lisa's hair, preventing her from walking away after a conversation that they were having was not going the way he had planned. I was very sad at the thought of going through another divorce, but with my oldest daughter's health and welfare my priority I decided the three of us would be better off without him.

Lisa was a wonderful helping hand for me, being ten years older than Lacey. I did have full-time daycare for Lacey at a local home, but on the days I was not able to bring her to the daycare, I would have either her father or Lisa babysit. But this was often stressful because he was not dependable. One day when I went to drop off Lacey at her dad's apartment, we went to his sliding glass door and knocked repeatedly without ever getting a response. We then went back home so I could have Lisa babysit.

It was a school vacation day and Lisa had spent the night at her friend's. I felt terrible, but I called her friend's house and talked to the friend's dad and explained the situation and asked him to wake Lisa up and let her know I was on my way over to pick her up so she could watch Lacey while I went to work. If she babysat Lacey all day for me, I would pay her for her time. Lisa never once complained about having a little sister she needed to help out with because I was a single mother.

Lisa, Lacey and I had many happy times together. We would turn on music in our living room, hold hands, dancing around the room, laughing and singing. Lisa loved fixing Lacey's hair or dressing her up, it was like she had a life-size Barbie doll. All of Lisa's girlfriends thought Lacey was so cute! Lacey was a very quiet girl so she was never an irritating younger sister.

When Lisa would have boys over in her room, I would send Lacey down to see what they were up to. Lisa had to keep her room door open when boys were in there so Lacey would just bounce in and out of Lisa's room and then come upstairs to give me reports.

Even though I had a baby when I was barely out of high school, I never regret having her. Yes, there were many difficult times, yet the priceless memories I have of the first time my girls walked or the first words they said are far above any hard times I had as a mother. After a difficult day of work, coming home to my daughters' sweet faces and listening to how their day went made the bad days better.

When my daughters were in dance, swimming lessons, choir,

softball and the list goes on…it brought me great joy to watch them grow and excel. If they fell down, I was there to pick them up and encourage them to try it again. Motherhood is my favorite occupation.

Chapter 7

Health and Addiction

*"Mom, I'm not going to share any
of your birthday cake with you."*

My stepdad was severely addicted to sugar. Throughout our childhood, he had such a severe sugar addiction that he would hide Pepsi all over the house, worried that he would run out. As a grade-schooler, I caught onto his sugar addiction. I could make chocolate chip cookies without using a recipe because I had it memorized. And this addiction carried on into my adult life. The sad thing is that sugar is actually the main ingredient in many items on grocery store shelves. If a manufacturer adds sugar to our food, we're more likely to consume it and become addicted, increasing their sales—as well as the risks to our health.

After the birth of my first child, Lisa, I was young, broke and alone with a baby who cried nearly all the time. I was on food stamps for about a year, during which I bought all kinds of good food like steak and vegetables, but I also bought ingredients to bake cookies and other sweets.

I was beyond exhausted, got almost no sleep, and had a husband that was never around. I cycled down into deep depression, which meant that my kitchen sink was usually filled with dirty dishes. My life was on autopilot; feeding and changing my baby, washing cloth diapers and doing laundry, cleaning and shopping for food and wondering why my baby would not stop crying. I would eat sweets to lift my moods, but that only resulted in a helter-skelter dive in my blood sugar, which made me want more; thus the cycle continued.

Once Lisa was a year old, I finally began to get some sleep and started to exercise. I joined a local athletic club, worked out, dropped a few pounds and felt better. I felt so great I stopped exercising, so I kept eating lots of sugar, regaining the weight I'd lost. Then I thought it would be a good idea to eat nothing but popcorn to lose weight. I limited myself to only popcorn, lost weight, felt a little bit better, stopped eating popcorn and resumed eating sugar, only to gain back the weight.

Another time my aunt introduced me to the concept of "miracle muffins." They consisted of stone ground wheat, molasses, raisins, cinnamon and nuts. I ate them all the time, lost weight, felt better, stopped eating miracle muffins, resumed my consumption of sugar and gained back all the weight I'd lost.

In my late 30s, still addicted to sugar and in poor health, I was sitting outside in the sun trying to combat a severe cold. By my side I had my phone, chicken noodle soup and a big multi-vitamin. I gently rocked back and forth on our deck swing. I loved the feel of the warm sun on my face. As I slurped my soup I reached for the horse-sized multi-vitamin next to me. I thought this pill should help, but unfortunately it was the worst thing I could have taken. Little did I know that the glands in my neck had reduced my swallowing capacity.

As I popped the huge pill in my mouth with some water, it immediately lodged in the back of my throat, completely cutting off my air supply. I panicked! I had to breathe or I would die! I doubled over trying to throw up, and when that did not work, I started thrashing my index finger down my throat in desperate effort to move the pill enough to get some air into my lungs. I was gouging the back of my throat with my fingernails, but I did not care, *I had to move that pill so I could breathe.* Finally the pill moved slightly and a small amount of air could pass through. I stayed doubled over and kept my mouth open, breathing the best I could and let my saliva drip out of my mouth. I stayed that way for a while, not really sure about the passage of time. Eventually I knew I would survive, but I needed to call for help.

I pushed my husband's quick dial link on my phone and was beyond relief when he answered.

"Hello, how is your cold doing?" Jim casually asked.

"I need you," is all I could barely squeak out.

"I am on my way!" Jim said quickly and the line went dead.

Jim was by my side in what seemed like just a few short minutes, and said he wanted to take me to the hospital. He helped me up and I slowly walked with my head hung down so the saliva could continue to drip out as I got into his truck. Jim handed me a napkin to collect the spit as he drove the 15 miles to the nearest hospital.

After we checked in at the hospital they did my vitals and drew some blood. The doctor looked in my throat and said it looked red, swollen, and the pill had dissolved. He also said my throat would be sore, and it would take time for the swelling to go down so I needed to be cautious with the food and drink I consumed. The results showed my blood's iron levels were at such a very dangerous level they wanted to give me a blood transfusion. I said absolutely not, I am strong and will get through this. When they realized they could not change my mind, they gave me a prescription for liquid iron and directions to take it two times a day until the bottle was empty, and sent me home.

When my parents heard about my day, they rushed over with what they call "goop." It's a mixture of lecithin, oats, wheat, yeast and maybe a few other things I do not recall. Mom said every morning she mixes this concoction with a powder breakfast packet, and drinks it for a day full of energy and health. I decided to give it a try because I knew my current diet was not giving me what I needed, and as a result I was sick.

I was still trying to figure out the whole healthy living way and hadn't quite mastered it yet when my body decided it had enough and was going to "talk" to me. I was outside of my body and had intense fear. Prior to this surge of fear that evening, I had been busy fixing our accounting software at work, moving my daughter out of her college dorm room and popping sweets like they were going out of style. When the fearful sensation attacked me in an instant, it was horrific. I felt like I was surely going to die any minute so I rushed to find my husband in the other room.

"I think I'm dying and I don't know what's going on." I said in a panic.

"You'll be okay, you're just having a panic attack. Remember your crazy day? This is your body trying to recover from it. I've had these before; you'll be all right. Let's go lie down on the bed. Take deep breaths and try to relax," my husband gently said.

My body very slowly came down from the intense fear and confusion. After what felt like hours, I said, "I'm sure glad that's over, I finally feel human again. I wouldn't wish a panic attack on my worst enemy."

Since this severe panic attack, I have had other mild attacks. Because I feel that my poor diet and too much stress caused my attack, I try to eat healthy and limit my stress as much as possible. When I feel stressed out, and I can feel the impending doom threatening, I run in place and flap my arms to use up the adrenaline. It may sound crazy, but it works for me, and I have never had a severe attack again.

My weight and health were on a roller coaster, up and down, depending on my diet. When the size of my waist was the same as my 36" inseam, I decided it was time to lose the weight once and for all. I had no idea how to stop the sugar addiction because I'd never been taught to eat healthy, but I was going to figure it out.

I started reading, researching and came across many helpful books. Shock is what I felt when I read *Sugar Savvy* by Kathie "High Voltage" Dolgin, and learned that I was starving myself. I was overweight, but my body was starved for all the nutrients it needed. The cookies and cakes were just packing on the fat and not satisfying the true need, so my body kept telling me to eat in the hopes it would get the proper nutrition it desperately wanted. The book is full of great tips: eat no more than 24 grams of sugar in 24 hours, kick your trigger foods to the curb, and that exercise is a natural mood booster, just to name of few that made sense to me.

The Gabriel Method by Jon Gabriel taught me the need to hydrate my body. It amazes me to think that we often mistake dehydration for hunger, and so many times we actually eat because we are thirsty. In the book, he suggests we drink two glasses of water first thing in the morning, a glass of water before each meal and a little more during the meal. I do try to do this, but have to admit I do fall short sometimes.

A few years ago, my daughter Lisa, who has always been aware of my battle with weight and sugar addiction, suggested we both try the 28-day clean-eating challenge through a nutrition/skincare/cosmetics company. This program gives a list of foods to eliminate from your diet as well as what to include. There are healthy meal recipes and a Facebook group for guidance and support. I agreed to give it a try because I had lost most of the weight, but still struggled with the last 40 pounds I was trying to lose.

I also battle with psoriasis. When I am not taking proper care of my body, it gives me a visual sign with spots similar to what I endured as a child. When I eliminate bad foods like sugar-loaded foods from my diet, my body will respond by having the psoriasis decrease. If I go on a binge and indulge in my wicked old ways of eating sugar and junk food, my psoriasis will flare up. Our bodies are amazing machines, and if we listen to them and give them the proper fuel, hydration, sleep and exercise, they will perform much better.

Sugar addiction is surprisingly a lot like alcohol addiction. I used to drive to the local gas station, buy a bag of cookies, eat them in the car, and then throw away the bag so no one would know I just ate three huge cookies. I would have been mortified if Jim peeked into my car and found cookie crumbs all over my seat.

Husband Jim often told me, "When I get the urge to drink, I turn it over to God." He has been sober since 2002—and occasionally still has thoughts of drinking. Some nights he will wake me and say, "Can we talk for a while? I just had one of those drinking dreams."

Jim's struggle with alcohol and how he overcame it has been helpful in my journey of sugar addiction. I have used some of his tools and tricks to help me deal with my addiction.

Jim showed me what he learned in Hazelden—to meditate and do deep breathing. With intentional quiet times of sitting or lying down, I get in touch with myself and with my higher power, God. When I live more for earthly pleasures like alcohol and sweets, I am more concerned with my next fix rather than my purpose in life.

During this time, I discovered a book by Allen Carr called *Good Sugar, Bad Sugar*. I read the whole thing on a short business trip, and it changed my life. I finally understood the difference between good sugar and bad, and how it affects the body and the way it functions. As a result, I began to make informed decisions about the kinds of food I ate, increased my activity level and added aerobic exercise and light weight-lifting, nothing extreme—but in the process the weight came off rather easily. I tried jogging, but it felt like torture, so I went back to using my elliptical machine that I enjoy.

Now, during the weeks when I am tired and too busy to exercise I can really tell the difference, and I eagerly look forward to getting back into the habit. It took me about a year to lose the final forty pounds, and I am happy to say I have maintained a healthy weight now for over two years. When I say I am healthy, I mean that I have some meat on my bones to keep me warm in the cold Midwest winters.

For me, one cupcake wakes up a gremlin inside me that just wants *more, more, more.* As a result, I have to keep tabs on myself and watch what I am eating. Looking back, I realize now that I was much moodier when I ate large amounts of sugar because it induced extreme highs and lows in my blood sugar that absolutely controlled my life. Another benefit of eating right and exercising is that I am rarely sick now.

I also took back the power I had given food. I used to go to food when I was looking for love or happiness. I did not truly love myself, and thought I was unworthy of love—and food filled that void. Over the past few years as I began to heal myself, with the help of God, I realized how much I depended on food. I now fill up with God's word and His love. *I am enough just as I am, God does not make mistakes.* I now wake up every morning and give thanks to God, for my health, His love, and whatever else I am grateful for at the time.

I use to think my stomach should feel really full, even stuffed, after I ate a meal. My old normal was feeling a bit of pain in my gut after eating. Once I started eating healthy, I would eat slower, felt satisfied and did not have an uncomfortable feeling in my gut. At first it felt strange. *Why don't I feel something in my stomach?* I asked myself after a meal. Then I thought about it. *So this is what my stomach sensation should be like after a nourishing meal?* Happiness and joy washed over me when I realized that I have overcome my addiction.

Jim and I are part of local church community that is helpful in guiding us on our Christian connection with God and in being Jesus's hands and feet on earth, spreading the good news to others as Jesus commissions us in Matthew 28:18-20. We are now full of God's love and the love from our family and friends so we do not feel the need to go back to our abusive addictions. We have Christian friends that also have a past of addictions, and we can discuss and talk openly about our pasts, where we have been and the changes we have made to encourage each other. With our focus on God instead of our addictions, it's made our life more stable and successful in life, family and business.

Recently Mom had her 81st birthday. I feel a birthday is not complete without a cake so I ordered a carrot cake with lots of sugary frosting. As I drove to see Mom I worried about what I was going to do. Should I eat a small bite of the cake? Maybe one piece? I did not want to get off my healthy lifestyle, and I felt like if I had some cake it would go the wrong direction again. I see people eating cake and sweets all the time without having issues; I am not one of them.

"Mom, I'm not going to share any of your birthday cake with you."

"Why in the world not? You love cake and it's my birthday!" she said with surprise.

"Mom, I have battled so long with sugar and I am in good health now I don't want to take the chance of ruining it."

"Okay, I will eat your piece for you!" Mom happily replied.

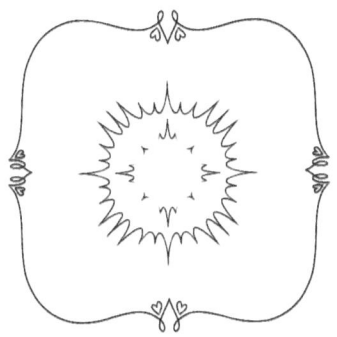

Chapter 8

Light in the Darkness

"For I know the plans I have for you," declares the Lord, "plans to prosper you and not to harm you, plans to give you hope and a future." Jeremiah 29:11

My mom has always been very religious. Whenever she was in a difficult situation, she would pray, "God, you need to take over, because I don't know what to do." Mom's life has been full of adversity. She had difficulty dealing with the early loss of her mom, her husband (my dad) leaving her, and the loss of her youngest son. Living the majority of her life without a mother left a large void in her daily life, and she felt alone most of the time. Her father was very active in the church and often brought her to church with him. Being in church, connecting with other Christians and learning more about Jesus was a highlight in Mom's life. When she was lonely, she would reach out to God and find comfort knowing He loved her unconditionally.

When my dad left our family, Mom was particularly lost and lonely. She drew on her strong faith to pull her through the struggle of learning how to be a single mother and sole provider. It was not easy for her, and she reached out to God often asking for guidance.

Today, although her memory is very poor regarding earthly things, God is still very clear to her. When I was a young adult, Mom would encourage me to go to Bible studies with her or give me the literature from a Bible study she'd attended. Now in her 80's she's still talking about God all the time.

I now spend a lot of my free time with Mom because I do not know how much time she has left on Earth. I often pick her up at her care residence and take her for a drive to in the countryside, and we stop by our cabin to see God's bountiful beauty in nature. She loves looking at all of the farms along the way and to reminisce about times past and her time in Iowa. She used to de-tassel corn and tells me about it each time we see a cornfield.

On one such outing, with the smell of cows and corn hanging in the air, we drove through the countryside and she chatted about all of the glorious animals and plants God put on earth. We talked freely about God and all that He has done for us.

We did not always have this kind of relationship; it has evolved over the years. I am happy how far we have come together, and feel a sense of peace that when her time is over and she goes to Heaven, I will have many fond memories to hold me over until I see her again.

Mom has guided me in the Christian way from my youth, just as her father taught her. My youth was enveloped in Christianity, but I had doubts along the way. When I had questions, I would ask Mom what she thought, and she was always happy to share her beliefs with me.

In 1974 Mom decided I was old enough, at age nine, to graduate to a "real" Bible from the one with large pictures on every page and few words that I had read up until that point.

As Mom was tucking me into bed, she handed me the red soft leather-bound Bible. When I opened it, I saw that she had written a prayer inside the front cover:

Light in the Darkness

Into my heart
Into my heart
Come into my heart
    Lord Jesus
Come in today
Come in to stay
Come into my heart
    Lord Jesus

    I have recited this prayer hundreds of times. Many times I repeated these words when I felt distant from God because of my own selfish behavior. Saying the words would make me feel better about what I was going through. I liked to think that I could make the words come to life, and that Jesus did actually come into my heart as I said them.

    I sometimes open that Bible and look at the poem. It helps when I am having a hard time dealing with Mom's failing health. I can look at her handwriting and remember back to the time when she was vibrant and sitting at my bedside in full health. The memory brings me comfort in my current situation of watching Mom decline and slowly slip away from me.

    When I need to remind myself that Mom's health was not always bad, I go back into my memories and recall our years together. One such memory is when we were allowed to ride our bikes to church. Mom normally drove us to church when we lived in Maplewood. When I was around 11, our family car was not working so we had to ride our bikes the five blocks to a close-by church because it was unthinkable that we would miss church.

    We loved riding our bikes because that meant we were on our own without adult supervision because Mom did not have a bike. So on that day, she stayed home. It's surprising that we made it to church and back without any trouble.

Causing trouble was what we did best as kids, and we did it often. Weekly Mom would get calls from the school telling her one of her kids was in the office again for misbehaving…or they would ask her if she knew where her kids were on the days we skipped school. I can't even imagine how much work it must have been trying to keep track of seven kids plus three foster teenagers each day! And yet Mom sent us to church without an earthly chaperone, which I think showed her faith. She must have been praying the whole time we were out. Her prayers were answered because we made it home safely.

Getting ready for this big event of riding to church by ourselves brought lots of energy to all of us. We ran down the steps to the garage and grabbed our bikes from the makeshift shed behind the garage. We bumped into each other as we all tried to get the bikes out the plywood double doors at the same time and the pedals kept getting hooked in the spokes of another bike. Big brother Todd was the most forceful and was trying to get out first, but his bike was at the back because he did not ride as much as the younger siblings did. We finally got the bikes out without any blood loss.

As we rode east on the county road towards the church, my brothers were riding slowly, enjoying the freedom and scenery. But I have always been in a hurry, and today was no exception. I enjoyed church, learning about Jesus and singing songs. I was pedaling hard, standing up on my bike pedals at the front of the pack.

"Hurry up you guys, we are going to be late for church!" I yelled at my brothers.

"Quit being so bossy, we have plenty of time!" Scott yelled back at me as my other siblings shook their heads.

Learning patience was a challenge for me. I have always been on the fast track wanting to get to my destination as quick as possible. Spirituality has been a part of me that has grown in importance and with that, the need to slow down, meditate on God's guidance and enjoy my surroundings that I am blessed with instead of always seeing it as a fast blur.

Growing in the church family, at age 12, we were required to learn in great detail what it meant to be a Christian. Each Wednesday during the school year Mom would drive me to our church for confirmation class. I had mixed feelings about going to the classes. I enjoyed learning more about Jesus, but some of the girls teased me because I wore makeup and appeared different.

At the end of the two years, getting ready to be confirmed, I had to decide what bible verse was most important to me and that I'd recite in front of the church. We were to wear a long white silky robe with a red carnation pinned to the lapel when we recited our verse. I chose John 3:16 as my bible verse because to me this verse sums up Christianity.:

*"For God so loved the world that he gave his one
and only Son, that whoever believes in him shall
not perish but have eternal life." John 3:16*

Jesus was perfect, without sin, yet he gave his life for us. In the Old Testament we read about the rules and Ten Commandments and how the people constantly screwed up. They would shed the blood of a lamb and repent as directed by God through Moses. Now all we have to do is believe Jesus's blood is enough. We all sin, but if we repent and believe, we can have eternal life.

The first time I remember sinning was when I stole a sticker. I was eight years old, and only recently trusted to go out alone on my bike, when I made my maiden voyage to a local drugstore just to look around. It was a gloomy Saturday morning, but nothing could dampen my excitement for riding to the store alone when Satan saw his chance to entice me. My adrenaline was running high when I arrived at the store, put my bike in the bike rack and entered another world filled with amazing new things to look at and buy. I looked around as the bright fluorescent lights lit it all up and made everything look irresistible. One entire shelf held a vast selection of shiny stickers that kept calling my name. *"Come here little girl. Come and take a closer look at us. So shiny and pretty."*

I picked up a sticker, looked at it and then put it back down. It was glistening under the bright lights when Satan whispered, *"Take it. They have so many no one will ever know."*

I turned back to look at the sticker as well as the other shiny items on the shelf. I should have walked away, but instead I stood there studying the endless rows of stickers and shortly caved in to temptation. I lifted my shirt slightly to sneak the sticker into the waistband of my pants. Just then the salesclerk walked to the end of my aisle and the two of us stared at each other. I knew the jig was up, but Satan had one more trick up his sleeve.

He whispered to me, cut your losses and run, no one would ever catch you. I zipped out of the store, slid onto my bike and fast-pedaled home. I was panting and sweating from the hard work of pedaling for three endless blocks.

Once I was safely at home, I took out the sticker, but I could not justify what I'd done, so I yelled at the devil. "How dare you make me do this? It's wrong!"

I entered the house where I went to find my mother. Without wavering, I said, "Mom, I need to tell you something."

We walked into the living room, where I sat down and she looked at me. "What is it?"

I took out the sticker, showed it to her and blurted out, "The devil made me do it!"

My face was hot with anger at the devil and fear at what I had done. I was panicking not knowing what was going to happen now that I had admitted my sin.

Then Mom said, "You know you can't keep this, it's wrong, we have to return it right now."

We got in our white VW van and headed down the road to the store. During the drive my mind kept playing scenes of what was going to happen next. The salesclerk would call the police and I would have to go to jail. How long would I have to stay there? Was I going to get yelled at by the salesclerk?

As Mom was parking the van, my hands started to sweat and I could hardly breathe. We got out of the van, walked up to the store and opened the door. The salesclerk looked right at us. Then he scowled and lifted his hand up and pointed at me, saying loudly, "You! You stole a sticker! I should call the police right now!"

As I hid behind Mom, she said, "She's just a kid and didn't mean any harm. She knows she did wrong and that is why she is here to return it and apologize."

"I'm sorry and won't ever do it again." I said while I peeked my head from behind Mom.

Mom handed the clerk the sticker and said, "Please forgive her, she is a good girl and has never done anything like this before."

"She better not ever do it again or I will call the cops next time!"

We quickly left the store before he could change his mind and headed back home. Mom felt I had suffered enough and had learned not to do it again, so I was not punished more. After Mom put the van in the garage, I quickly went up to my room and thought to myself that I love my warm room, and I am sure the jail cell would have been cold.

Stealing was wrong, yet I did it anyway, even though I have never doubted if there was a God, and knew better. I was raised that there was a God, and I took it as fact. My relationship to God, however, was not always clear-cut. When I moved out of Mom's house, I made decisions based on what I wanted, with little concern about what the bible said. If I wanted to go out partying and skip church in the morning because I was too tired, that's what I did. I was what I now call a "convenient Christian." When it was convenient, I went to church. When it was convenient, I read the Bible. I wish I could say I read the bible and found great wisdom in it at this time of my life. Usually if I was going to read the Bible I would do it in the morning before my day started, but the readings were few and far in between.

When I was pregnant with my second daughter, our church was in need of Sunday school teachers. When I heard the announcement, for some reason it called out to me and made me want to help so I decided to offer my assistance and teach a class. Mom led by example and was always helping others when she could. At church she would sing in the choir, be on a prayer chain, or encourage someone when they were in a tough spot. I did not knowingly follow Mom's example, but looking back she gave me a good foundation to lean into.

Getting ready to teach Sunday school was an adventure for my oldest daughter and me. We would read the week's theme and bible story, then go to the store and buy craft supplies so we could bring the stories to life for the kids in my class. When the story was about Adam and Eve, we tried to make clothes out of felt leaves and created snakes out of pipe cleaners. To show the story about Daniel in the lion's den, we made ferocious lions out of wire, cardboard and yarn. We would make an example of the craft together at home, and then bring it on Sunday to share with the kids.

Mom instilled in me that as a Christian I needed to have my girls baptized, so that is what I did when they were one month old. I thoughtfully considered who would be best suited to be the godparents for my girls. They had to believe in God and be close to the girls so they could assist with the religious education. For Lisa's godparents, I asked my brother Mike and his wife Laura, and for Lacey, her godparent is her older sister. Because of the 10-year-age difference I knew Lisa would always love and guide her younger sister. During the baptism, we were given candles that were to be lit for a few moments each year on their baptism date, and take time to renew the baptism vows and pray, thanking God for the grace given to us. We did light the candles for a few years after the baptism, but then the tradition slowly fell by the wayside.

When my kids got older they had sports, music, and dance to keep up with. These times were hectic and happy all at the same time, and my life felt full, even brimming. But that also meant I left God in the back seat of my life. I went through the motions of church but I did not feel any strong faith. It was just what we did, but I did enjoy seeing and visiting with the other church members.

There were some moments where God did feel close. Times when I would go on women's retreats with a group from church, I could feel God was near. On the retreats we encouraged each other to intentionally seek God. The retreats would have a specific theme with teachings around that theme. We would take a bus or carpool to a freezing cold (especially when the heater broke) YMCA in northern Minnesota so we could cross country ski and snowshoe, or rent a quaint old home or go to a retreat center on a lake that had a breathtaking view. The gathering would always be in a remote location to help you unwind and put the daily demands on hold.

One memorable retreat was a study on Esther. We broke into small groups and dove deeper into what being courageous looked like, and what it would have been like to be a woman in her time period. In the evening we had dinner together and stayed up late playing games like Uno, and everyone felt free to tell stories and laugh. Our friendships would blossom while spending quality time with other each other. I am not a social butterfly by any means, but I enjoyed meeting as many of the women as possible. During the day between learning sessions we would take walks in small groups, be real and talk about life in an open and honest way that's hard to do when you have constant daily life demands on you.

As I matured I began to read my bible often and discovered that I actually enjoyed it. I began to connect more deeply with the readings. When I read the book of John, I imagined what it would have been like to see Jesus change water to wine, His first miracle. I enjoyed reading other stories in the bible where Jesus and his disciples seem more like normal people, like you and me. I think back to the story in Matthew where Jesus calls out to Simon and Peter who were fisherman and says, "Come, follow me, and I will make you fishers of men." It made me feel like Jesus could just as well have called out to me. Simon and Peter were not anything special at that point; they appeared to be average men. But Jesus wanted them, maybe because they were regular people with regular daily problems so that others would be able to relate to them. They were like you and me, regular people with regular daily problems that can learn from Jesus and his teachings. Simon and Peter walked daily with Jesus and learned from Him, and then were able to teach others the good news in a language that was understandable to the average person.

Every day my husband needs to keep his struggle with alcohol in check. When he turns over the drinking desires to God, he feels God gives him the gift of sobriety. He is able to abstain from alcohol, but still has thoughts of it so it's not totally gone, just under control. Alcoholics Anonymous program refer to a higher power, which many of them believe is the Christian God, but they make it clear that it could be anything you know to be greater than yourself.

The higher power concept has been life changing for us because we used to depend on our own strengths to pull us through the adversity. We now surrender our life fully to God, asking for His strength and guidance to bring us through the hard times. I remind myself when I am in the middle of a challenge that I am in training, strengthening myself for my purpose. We stopped trying to control the outcome and let the outcome be God's. We try to do the best we can and let the outcome be His. We fully understand that timing is key; our timeline means nothing to God. He is all knowing and will deliver what we need at the right time.

To help our journey we bought a book through Hazelden's book-

Light in the Darkness

store—and have replaced it once already because the first one was worn out. Our current copy of *Twenty-Four Hours a Day* that I hold in my hand is a black hardcover, with smudges on the cover's title, water stains throughout, pages wavy and bent from excessive use. It has an earthy smell from all of the travels it's been on with us. The book has daily readings that are always thought-provoking. Whether from an alcoholic's perspective or a person without an alcohol addiction, the pages are insightful and makes you stop, and consider its words and how you can apply them to your life. The topics range from soul-sickness, thankfulness, ignoring evil instead of combating it, to serenity. Today's reading is on quietness, which is a perfect topic for me to study since I am always going at a fast speed. I do work on this because during the quiet times, the times I am intentionally seeking Him in the stillness, is the only time I feel God leading and guiding me.

Now that I am eager to know God intimately, I notice that He shows up all the more. While working on this book, God has showed up countless times. I will be working on a section, get stumped, slow down and meditate, and then the words will flow much easier from my fingertips to the keyboard. When I have a problem and need another's perspective, I will discuss it with my husband, knowing that he is a faithful believer and always has my best interest in mind—I feel God guides our conversations. Sometimes when I feel lost, I will go to YouTube and watch a sermon from one of my favorites like Elevation Worship or Mosaic, and my path will become clear. God shows up in many ways when I seek Him.

The majority of the time guidance comes through His word. But, when I was 52, God decided to reveal Himself to me in a more obvious way. Life had become very different for me. I was sober and my partying days were over. I was finally in a position to get to know God on a personal level without all of the guilt and shame over the previous night's mishap. The more I sought God through prayer and readings, the more I found Him. It was around this time I began to struggle with tremendous bleeding, in a women's way. It went on for two weeks and required many trips to the bathroom. Though I attributed it to menopause, I was beginning to worry how long this would continue. I made a doctor's appointment for the following day. That night I went to bed with my husband as we usually do, but what happened that night was far from normal.

With my husband sleeping soundly at my side, I noticed my heart began beating extremely fast, and I thought maybe I was having a heart attack. Confused, not knowing what symptoms of a heart attack really were, and not being sure what was happening, I just laid there perfectly still. My heart continued to beat very rapidly. I had lost a massive amount of blood over the past couple of weeks and thought it might be related to that. Was I going to die next to my husband? I was very scared, unsure what was happening. So scared, I was frozen in place.

Just then a bright ball of white light suddenly appeared in my room and startled me, because it was something I had never seen before and had no concept of what it was. The illuminated ball had small spikes coming out of all the surfaces about an inch or two long, in all directions and was not smooth, but rough and uneven. The overall diameter of the ball was about twelve inches. Quickly and quietly the bright ball came towards me from across the room, enveloping me. When the light was upon me, my heart suddenly resumed its normal rhythm and the bleeding abruptly stopped—the ball of light instantly disappeared, it did not travel back from where it came from, it just disappeared after it healed me.

It felt like a miracle. I lay in bed silently reliving what had just happened, and not sure what to do next. Should I wake my husband? Should I go to the hospital? But then the next thing I knew it was morning. I must have fallen asleep. Rising from bed, I felt better than I had in weeks. I remembered the events of the previous night, but I chose to keep it to myself. *Who would believe me anyway,* I thought. I called and canceled the doctor's appointment. I wondered if it had been a temporary fix, that the bleeding might start again, or that my heart would race uncontrollably again. It never did.

That night was not the only time I experienced a healing force. About two weeks later I came down with a severe cold. Day after day, it kept getting worse, even in spite of every effort to treat it myself. After a few days of feeling very sick, during the darkness of night, another bright ball of white light appeared. It was very similar to the other bright ball of light, with one exception. The bright light's intensity was slightly dimmer than the first time. The ball still had the same pointy surface, same diameter, but was less bright. It again came from the west, across the room and came towards me quickly and quietly, enveloping my body, making me well in an instant and then abruptly disappeared. I kept this miraculous event a secret again for a long time.

I have no idea why God chose to heal me twice, but I am wondering if it wasn't so I could glorify Him every chance I get. It has taken courage for me to share my story. At first I convinced myself that no one would believe I was healed by God twice. But, I then thought, *Why would God trust me with anything else if I did not have faith that the healing could benefit others as well as myself?*

As I was trying to understand these events, I picked up the Bible and came upon a passage in James.

"Every good and perfect gift is from above, coming down from the Father of the heavenly lights, who does not change like shifting shadows" James 1:17.

This struck me as God's word confirming that it was He who healed me. It brought me joy to know that the healing light had indeed been from Him, and that He chose to heal me. I feel a tremendous honor to be able to say God healed me. It shows me that He loves me, despite the regret and guilt I still carry. For many years I thought because of my divorces and my past choices I was doomed to hell, but why would He heal me if He did not forgive me and love me?

I have become convinced that God loves and forgives me, as He loves and forgives each one of us.

After these miraculous moments I sought to find God all the more. Once I started to consciously seek Him, He was easier to find. I began to realize that it was not Him who moved, He was always there, and it was me moving towards Him. I cannot get enough of God. I pray, meditate, read the Bible, listen to speakers and read books all in an effort to get closer to God.

As I started to become closer to God, I reflected on the years I was not close to Him. There were many times I thought only of my earthly life without any real consideration for what I was doing, and whether it was beneficial to the ever-after in Heaven. Sometimes I think I would like a do-over of the past, but then I stop myself and reflect on where those years have brought me. I now appreciate what I have learned from those events.

My life was not easy because of my skin condition, but it taught me how to treat people with respect no matter how they look. My divorces taught me how to live a faithful, happy life with my present husband.

Now, with God as my co-pilot instead of big piles of sugar and bottles of alcohol, life has become more rewarding and full of adventure. With a clear and sober mind, I found that I am able to quietly listen to God through His word and through the Holy Spirit that nudges me from within to make better choices and branch out of my comfort zone. Because God gave me a solid foundation of love and acceptance to fall back on, I felt able to go on adventures, to start businesses, to seek thrills in the sky and on the racetrack. People may worry that they will become a boring person without alcohol. Well, if jumping out of airplanes, driving a motorcycle, or racing cars is boring, then I guess I am. I became a happier and more confident person with God at the center of my life. I learned how to live my dreams.

You do not have to be a thrill seeker like me to enjoy life. Beauty is all around us and is free. Watching a waterfall or diving into the water can be a very soothing and beautiful experience. Imagine, the water is ever moving yet always in front of you. The flower is full of color, yet has an aroma that is beyond words. A tree is full of strength and power, yet only moves when the invisible wind pushes it. Enjoy life and take chances when you feel the spark inside of you that's bursting to come out.

Psalm 118:22 speaks beautifully about the stone that the builders had rejected has now become the capstone that holds the arch together. We who feel rejected can become mighty and strong, and rejoice and be glad because we will make a big impact in this world in spite of past rejections or mistakes.

I know God has big plans for you and me.

Chapter 9

Dreams Come True

*"Think of beautiful butterflies and the complete
metamorphosis they go through before they can grow
wings and soar to their full potential."*

When I was a young girl, I actually had high hopes of one day becoming President of the United States. Perhaps because I was always seeking acceptance, I felt being President would be the ultimate acceptance. Or perhaps it's because I have always liked being right and having everyone do things my way. Either way I still enjoy being in charge and being the president of our roofing company. I know I do not have all of the answers, and need to depend on our team to get the jobs done. We need a variety of personalities and different talents to get the work completed. Our employees all have past experiences, and they bring the best of them forward so we can satisfy our customer's needs.

A job I always thought I would enjoy was modeling. When I was ten years old, Mom enrolled me in a modeling class at a local department store. I was elated to be in that class where we learned about makeup, clothing and of course, how to walk the runway like professional models.

We were each encouraged to choose an outfit from the store, we styled our hair and put on makeup, then modeled the clothes in front of our parents and friends. I had a blast that day. I was on top of the world, feeling truly beautiful, because my world suddenly opened up, offering possibilities I'd never previously considered. Maybe there was hope for this spotted girl after all; maybe I could really become a model.

Over the years my jobs have taken many twists and turns. Delivering phone books in a baby carriage works well if you're poor and in desperate need of money. That was one of my many jobs when I was a young mother trying to make ends meet. When that no longer paid enough, I worked as an apartment manager for a time in exchange for free rent. But I found out early on that managing the needs of the tenants in my building was a difficult task.

My favorite was the guy who decided to haul motorcycle parts up to his fourth-floor apartment where he assembled them in his living room. I never found out exactly how he managed to get that mammoth motorcycle down four flights of stairs and out the front door. I did not miss the endless cleaning, repairs and yard work when I left it all behind and moved to Minnesota.

After the move, I was trying to carve out a career for myself. I got my first factory job when I was 20 after convincing Human Resources that they should hire me because my older brother Mike had previously worked there and had done an excellent job. The company sorted stamps and packaged them for the US Postal Service. My fingers were so moist that the stamps kept sticking to them, which meant that I was not a good fit for the job. Because I was a good employee, they asked me if I'd like to transfer to the Quality Control department. I jumped at the opportunity and have enjoyed the chain of events that this created.

I was happy, but I found myself dreaming of advancement in the quality control field, so I began to apply at other companies. I eventually landed another job for more money, at a medical manufacturing company. While I was happily working there, my oldest brother Todd recommended me for a job at his company where I landed a manager position in their quality control department. That was a huge advancement for me, but the company was not one where I wanted to stay long-term, so I gained experience there and then started scouting for my next advancement.

I made an unwise decision when I faxed my resume using my current employer's fax machine to another company that was hiring, and a co-worker saw me and squealed to my boss. As a result, I was fired, but was blessed to be hired instantly by another company where I made more money. During those years I continued to move from one job to another at different companies in the quality control field where I acquired a great deal of valuable experience.

Learning all that I could in each of my positions was my kind of education since I did not have a college degree. I consumed as much information and training as I could, and once I felt I had gained as much from the position as I could, I would get bored and needed a new challenge. Applying for new jobs was great fun for me. I enjoyed updating my resume, scouting out new opportunities and meeting new people.

After about 18 years in the Quality Assurance field I decided to apply for a Quality Manager position at a large corporation in Menomonie, Wisconsin. I was invited to come in and discuss the open position. When I was interviewing with the hiring manager he mentioned I should become an ASQ Certified Quality Engineer (ASQ CQE). This certificate is given by the American Society for Quality (ASQ) signifying the individual is an expert in setting up and maintaining, management and quality control systems—and auditing systems for deficiency identification and correction.

After I looked into it, I had to agree that it looked like a great opportunity. By that time, I'd become burned out at my current job, so I reduced my work hours to allow more time to study for the exam. I organized my notes, read many books and diligently studied for nearly nine months. ASQ offered various locations to take the exam so I arranged to take the exam in Milwaukee, Wisconsin because I was excitedly planning to be in nearby Madison for the college graduation of my oldest daughter that same weekend. About two weeks after taking the exam, I received notice that I'd passed the exam and was officially certified, I could hardly contain my excitement and told everyone who would stand still long enough to listen.

During the same time I was studying to be an ASQ CQE, I was driving home from work in June of 2006, when my husband called to ask what I thought about starting a roofing company. He was already in the roofing industry and had many connections so it seemed like a good idea. I knew he was good in his trade, and my management experience would be a good fit for starting a company.

Being the owner of a company appealed to me because over the years I preferred to be the one in charge, making the decisions instead of others. In my past positions my bosses would tell me to do something, but I usually felt there was a better, different way to do it. When I would voice my opinion, I would be looked at as a troublemaker for not wanting to do it their way. I would do my best to keep my mouth closed as much as possible, unless it was way off track; then I would have to say something.

Throughout my life I realized many of the traumatic situations did not damage or weaken me—*in fact the opposite was actually true.* The stories prove to me that I can get through hard times, and it gives me trust in my ability to move forward. I chose not be traumatized, but rather I choose to believe I got through the past trials and gained confidence.

I share my stories here so you can know that you can also get through your challenges to become a better, stronger person, and win at life.

With our own company, I would have the freedom to make the decisions and also have flexible hours. Our income would depend on the time we put into it, so we could decide our future. We officially opened our new roofing business in June of 2006. I became the president with my husband as the vice-president.

In the beginning we worked at our day jobs, and then did roofing during evenings and weekends. But it was not long before it really took off and began to grow by leaps and bounds. Soon after we started the business, my husband wanted to go fulltime with it, and we opened a second location in a nearby city and added employees. Because we needed health insurance, I kept my engineering job and benefits. But after some time, the roofing company was doing so well, and I was taking on so much work that we felt it was time for me to quit my second job. I went fulltime at our company, doing the accounting and working on sales while my husband and his team handled the roofing jobs.

Our company has done well, and we have already outgrown three previous locations and are now extremely happy in our fourth location. At first it was just Jim and me, but in order to grow our company to new higher levels, we needed to grow our team. We are pleased that we have a topnotch team and value and appreciate all that we have accomplished together. I consider our team an extended family. We are close, and when they have their own personal family needs, we work together as a team to allow flexibility, and we still give quality product to our customers, and do it on schedule. It brings me joy to have a company that is able to hire hardworking, amazing employees that help us achieve our goals.

With our roofing company in a good place, I began dreaming of opening a store called the Pink Moose Boutique. My husband had previous roofing experience and was known in our community as the roofer, so most people assumed our roofing company was his alone, even when I put in many long days. With the boutique, it would give me my own identity.

I spent many hours attending fashion shows, retail apparel trade shows and researching the best retail practices. Craigslist was my best source for the tables, chests, mirrors and dressers I needed for the store. If Craigslist did not offer the things I needed to display the merchandise, I would negotiate great deals from a used-fixture store.

After several months of hard work, I pulled everything together and opened the new store with a big grand opening event, complete with a local guest celebrity. We had pizza from a local pizzeria. The customers enjoyed the games, prizes, smiles and discounts we offered. It was a great start to a new adventure.

My biggest challenge came with finding good, reliable employees to operate the boutique while I worked at the roofing company. Often employees would call in sick and could not work, and I'd have to drop everything and cover for them. When my store manager announced she wanted to go into another line of work and quit, I decided it was time to have a huge sale and close the store. I was sad to see my hard work come to a close, but I felt I was spread too thin owning two demanding businesses—and accepted the fact it was time to close the boutique. I miss the store because it was an extension of me. I had poured my heart and soul into setting up that store. From the pink walls to the pink mannequins, it was my dream that I shared with my employees and customers.

I had fun at the end-of-business sale where everyone was in great spirits while adding items to huge piles of merchandise they wanted to buy at 75 percent off retail. Within two weeks I'd sold everything in the store, including the furniture and fixtures. Shutting the back door to the store for the last time pulled terribly at my heart. I still miss going to the store and trying on the latest clothes, taking pictures for Instagram and Facebook to promote the store and talking to the customers.

Funny how over the years certain conversations will stick in your mind while others seem to pass right through. I remember a couple times in my life when I was told I should be a model. They happened when I was about 19.

"Hey pretty lady, can I take your photo? You look like a model!" A guy I didn't know yelled at me as I walked past him in the park.

Laughing, I replied, "You're crazy, I am no model!"

He countered very matter of fact, "Actually, I do know what I'm talking about as I'm a professional photographer."

I laughed and kept walking, telling myself, *No way do I look anything close to a model.*

The second time it was from a friend who was in the modeling business.

Marnie looked at me seriously one day as we were having lunch together and said, "You are beautiful Leslie, you would be a great model."

Stunned, I replied, "No one would want to hire me, I'm no model."

Looking back trying to remember the remainder of the conversation, I recall that I couldn't let myself believe the possibility of being a model. My self-doubt sabotaged any chances of it becoming a reality.

If I was a model, then I was found appealing by others and was accepted. I didn't accept myself as worthy; therefore, it wasn't in my realm of possibility to allow myself to think others might find me attractive. With my experiences as a spotted little girl, I was looked at sometimes with curiosity and cruelty when I was seeking consent of acceptance. My low self-esteem from being spotted haunted me for years.

After many, many years without anyone teasing or staring at me because of spots, I began to slowly gain self-confidence. A couple of years ago a friend suggested a photographer take photos of me so I could create a portfolio and present it to modeling agencies. I was finally now in a place where I started to believe others might find me attractive. I followed up and scheduled a photo shoot with the photographer. We hit it off, became friends and she ultimately recommended me to a modeling agent she was currently using which she thought would be a good fit for me.

I sent photos of myself to the agent and waited a couple of weeks for a response. I received an email asking me to come to her studio for a meeting. With my carefully made-up face, hair and outfit on, I drove to Minneapolis for the appointment. Standing outside of the building in my high heels, looking up at the old brick building, brought me joy. Maybe I was okay after all.

The meeting went great, and I was asked to be one of the models their customers could consider for projects. That day it felt like the agent was telling the little girl inside of me "you are beautiful, you are accepted."

The first time my agent sent me an email for an audition for a customer's new beauty line, I was very excited, until I read the part about submitting a photo for consideration wearing *no makeup,* and specified that I would be required to audition with "No/None/Zero/Zilch" makeup on my face. I had worn makeup since the fourth grade, and I could count on my fingers how many people have seen me without it. I felt shaky even thinking about going without makeup because it was like asking me to walk naked down Main Street.

Reeling from my first opportunity at being a model and not sure what to do, I left my computer in search of my husband and found him in the kitchen.

"Honey, my agent wants me to audition for a new beauty line, but I don't want to do it," I said as I helped him prepare dinner.

"Why not? You've been waiting for this opportunity," Jim reminded me as he passed me the cooking pan.

"Yeah, but I want to do fashion, not makeup," I said like I had other modeling options.

"You have to start somewhere," he encouraged me, knowing I didn't have any other offers.

"I guess you're right. I'll do it," I said more bravely than I felt as I dumped the chicken in the pan for dinner.

After we ate, I walked into our bathroom and washed my face to remove all of my makeup, took a selfie and submitted my photo via email to be considered for the audition. A few days later I received a reply email saying: Yes! They wanted me to audition. I was flattered they thought I looked good enough, even without makeup, to be a model, which gave me a huge boost in my confidence.

Nervous and excited I headed to the audition wearing no makeup. I was looked at, asked to turn this way, that way, in the bright light. I survived. I did it and no one laughed at me. Of course, the spots on my face are now quite faded and scarcely visible at all. But in my mind's eye, they're still bright red just as they were when I was a child. My arm did have psoriasis on it, and was noticed when they applied one of the moisturizers on it that they were advertising. Since the moisturizer was not able to mask the psoriasis, this may answer why I was not offered the job. Even though I initially told my husband I did not want to audition, I was still disappointed I was not selected for the commercial.

We learn each and every time we try something, even when the outcome is different than originally expected. Stepping out of our comfort zone can be overwhelming because stretching our potential sometimes is painful, but as you grow, the pain becomes your victory. Think of beautiful butterflies and the complete metamorphosis they go through before they can grow wings and soar to their full potential. They start as an egg, become a caterpillar, eat lots of food and grow. During this growth period they grow so much they have to shed the outgrown skin several times. Next they create a chrysalis and within these walls they undergo a remarkable transformation. Can you image changing your entire body in a cramped cell? That must be painful! But, look at the beautiful creature that emerges from the chrysalis and what it is now able to accomplish because of the change it endured. The butterfly can now fly from flower to flower or from tree to the sky and back again. It can soar to its heart's desire because of what its endured. I challenge you to act like a caterpillar and become your best version.

Chapter 10

Racing Towards Joy

"'I did it!' I'm screaming in my head when I cross the finish line first and the checkered flag is waving!"

Years ago, I dreamed of being a racecar driver. NASCAR would have been great, but I am fine with the local dirt track where I have been racing. About seven years ago, one of our friends let me drive his racecar, and I enjoyed it so much that my husband surprised me with my very own red Dodge Neon racecar.

Racing is a wonderful outlet for me where I can go crazy fast, and learn to trust myself and the car through lots of practice time on the racetrack.

In the beginning I was apprehensive about driving a car fast on the oval dirt track. My first time racing I was not concerned with winning the race, I just wanted to finish the race. Embarrassing as it was, I was lapped—passed by all the other cars. As I drove around the track with the other cars, I was not sure how fast I could go without tipping the car over on the corners. I drove slowly and did not tip over, drove faster, did not tip over, so I kept going faster and faster until I caught up with the other cars and no longer was being lapped. I did not come in last place my first time racing. One of the other cars had engine trouble and could not finish the race, so on the posted results I finished the race second to last.

Now, getting my car on the trailer to head out to the racetrack gets my excitement going. I can't eat any food hours before the race because my whole body is on high alert. Once at the track it's important to draw the right number for determining the car's position in the line-up. I always hope for the lowest number so I will be in pole position and start the race.

As I watch the class of cars race before me, I excitedly put on my fire retardant pants, jacket and shoes. I turn on my RACEceiver and put my earbuds in so I can hear what the control tower is saying.

"You better get into your car and get in line," my husband says.

"Yep, I don't want to miss the race!"

I grab my helmet, neck brace, and gloves and head for my car. I slide through the space where the window has been removed and adjust my bottom into the tight-fitted seat. I try to find all of my five harnesses and get them untwisted and adjusted. My husband reaches in and helps me line them up in proper position and correct tightness. Once lined up, I securely latch them together at my crotch. I put my neck brace, helmet, and gloves on and start the car's engine. I also push down the pedal a few times to make some noise and listen to her roar.

I push in the clutch, shift into first gear, give it some gas and head out to our lineup at the track entrance. My heart begins to beat a little faster, and my whole body starts to shake with excitement. We are staring at the traffic light waiting for it to turn green so we can enter the track. I give the guy next to me a thumbs up and he gives me one back. We rev up our engines to show we are ready. The green light illuminates, and taking turns, we head out in single file to the bumpy, wet, dirt track. We get in our starting position line-up, pull up behind the pace car and stop. The pace car slowly starts out and we do a warm-up lap; then the pace car exits and we keep rolling around the track until the green flag is waved—and then it is *PEDAL to the METAL!*

It's all-out war! I want to be on the inside track and will do anything to keep that position. Going as fast as possible on the straight-aways, only slightly slowing down for the corner, then I gun it again halfway through the corner to come out fast and furious.

I did it! I am screaming in my head when the checkered flag is waving as I cross the finish line first in my red Dodge Neon racecar. *Woo-hoo!* I thought, *Satisfaction at its finest!*

The announcer said: *"And the winner is…Leslie Jackson."*

I drove to victory lane, stopped, unbuckled, slid out of my car window, took off my helmet, shook my long mane of hair, and stood next to my car waiting for my trophy. The announcer did a double take and looked at me with shock and disbelief because I was a woman, saying, *"And she even has blonde hair."* Everyone cracked up laughing.

Now a few years later, while looking at my new white Monte Carlo race car I wondered: why had it been a good idea to sell my red Dodge Neon that I had won races with—and buy a different class car that I have no clue how to race? When I look at my white racecar as it sits on the trailer in our driveway, it has the required sponsor stickers on the rear side panels and the big number 12 proudly displayed on the doors, like it was important. The car has a dent in the front left fender from my last race because a few of us were trying to get ahead in the pack and had a minor altercation.

My first race with the Monte Carlo I admitted to the women in registration that I had bought a new car and would be jumping up two classes from the Hornets to the Street Stocks—and I had absolutely no idea how to race this car. I wanted them to put me at the back of the pack, so I could practice, get to know my new car, and not slow others down or get in their way and cause an accident.

When Jim and I unloaded the car at my first race, I felt awkward. What was the tire pressure of these bigger tires supposed to be? Where was that sheet of paper where I had my notes telling us what the psi should be? Finally we got everything figured out and the car was ready for the race. Was *I* ready? That was entirely a different question. I felt like everyone was staring at me, a lady, who was going to race with all of those men who could get their cars ready with their eyes closed. They skillfully drove their Street Stock cars. They knew what they were doing…I did not.

When it was our turn to race, we slowly rolled onto the dirt track, and I was last, safely out of the men's way. We kept rolling around the track at a slow speed, making sure everyone was in their proper starting position, and waiting for the voice in our ear to tell us we would be making the final lap before the race would begin. My body tingled with excitement at the anticipation of the first race. When the pole setter, which is the car at the inside front row, reached the orange cone, the flagman waved his green flag, and the stoplight turned green, and the race began. As we all put the pedal to the metal and started racing, I was scared and thrilled all at the same time to be on the track driving a car I had no clue how to race. This car was rear-wheel drive, and my Neon had been front-wheel drive, so it was not cornering the same at all. I started to spin in corner #3, I let my foot off the gas, quickly adjusted for the spin by turning the steering wheel and came out of it okay. I gave it gas and shot forward along the stretch in front of the fans, thinking, *At least I am giving them something to watch, and hopefully I don't crash.*

My love for driving fast and maneuvering the curves began the first day I received my driver's license. The thrill of racing, making split-second decisions, and the roar of the engines all bring me excitement that can only be fueled on the racetrack. I know the smell, dirt and noise is not for everyone, and that's okay. We are all unique, and I do not try and push my passion on others, except for my husband. He doesn't enjoy racing like I do, but I need him to be my pit crew. Racing is very much a team sport. I need a mechanic for the endless repairs, and I am also thankful for everyone that helped by giving guidance on what to do on the track. And without the fans the track would not be sustainable, so many thanks to them.

I am pleased to have been able to take first place twice in the Hornets division, and have two trophies to show for it. Both times I won, the other drivers were all men, which gives me a great feeling of self-worth since it is rare for a lady to race cars, let alone win. It can be hard living and working in arenas that are male-dominated. I know this from my roofing company as well as from racing. It's true that initially women do not always get treated the same as men. When thoughts of unfairness pop into my head, I do not let it control me, but rather it pushes me to be even better. In the places I show up, I do my best, hold others accountable as well as myself, and demand respect.

Thinking back to my childhood days of itchy red spots, to now being able to race cars, it just goes to prove adversity doesn't have to keep you in the back seat of your life. You can take control and make your dreams come true no matter what life throws at you.

For my 50th birthday in 2015 I wanted to do something even bigger than when I went skydiving—so I decided to drive a real NASCAR vehicle. "Chicagoland" in Joliet, Illinois, offered a 28-lap Richard Petty driving experience in an authentic NASCAR vehicle. I asked a few people if they wanted to go with me. No one did, so I went by myself.

Going on this adventure solo made it even more fun. No one was there to consult with on how the weekend would play out. I decided when to leave, when to stop, what to eat, what music to listen to, when to go to bed, and when to get up. I decided to drive down the day before the big event so I could relax and enjoy my stay. I rented a hotel room close by the track because I did not want to be late for *the experience of a lifetime.*

The day of the race was bright, clear, with lots of sunshine. We had a class before we were allowed out on the track. Once the class was finished we had to wait for our turn. As I watched others go around the track, I started to get excited. Finally it was my turn. I signed up to have my picture taken with the car so we did that first while my hair still looked good and I didn't yet have helmet head. I got comfortable in my seat and my instructor sat in the passenger seat next to me.

"Are you ready?" the instructor asked routinely.

"I've been ready for this all my life!" I declared, my face beaming with excitement.

"Okay then, slowly go straight and safely merge onto the track, there are others on the track, and we don't want any collisions," he warned.

I let the clutch out and began the "race." I quickly adjusted to driving this car rather than my dirt track car and was over 100 mph in no time.

"Looks like you know what you are doing," he noticed, grinning.

"I drive dirt track, so this is familiar to me," I said proudly.

"You shouldn't have any problems then."

He gave me pointers about when to drop down from the high side to the lower portion of the track as we entered the corner so I could still maintain a fast speed—yet keep control of the car. *I better listen to him or I will roll this sucker,* I thought.

The instructor wore a headset and communicated with the other instructors on the track.

"Number 30, we are closing in, please move down a lane," he warned the car in front of us.

I was running at speeds close to 170 mph so they let me have the run of the track, and had the slower cars move out of my way as I approached. Nothing better than going full throttle!

That once-in-a-lifetime experience was truly a dream come true for me, making me feel that I could do whatever I set my mind to do. My past, my present, all of my experiences have shaped me into the person I have become. Fearless? Brave? Basically my experiences have given me the confidence to trust my decisions and know that if I make a wrong turn, it's still okay, I can make changes, adjust my course, and still finish the race.

Even though it's been challenging writing this book, it also has been a time of great healing as I have worked through all that has happened to me over the years. Repressed feelings surfaced when I started to write about the different events of my hidden shame. *It's amazing how talking and writing about my past has actually been freeing. I thought my shame and guilt needed to be hidden, but the opposite has actually been true.*

I see authors becoming speakers and feel that might be a good next step for me too. I was so excited to receive my first email asking me to speak at a women's monthly gathering. I started to think: What will I wear? What should I say? Then, I started second guessing myself and feeling inadequate. Why do I think my story is worth sharing? *"No one will care about your story,"* I heard in my head. But, then I pushed the negative thoughts out of my mind and countered, *"I will tell my story, share my struggles, so others can know they are not alone, they too can change course, and drive into the victory lane."*

Trying to decide what would be the most powerful, meaningful words for these women to hear I wrote out two different speeches, but I crumpled up and threw both away. I thought back to Psalm 81:10 *Open wide your mouth and I will fill it.* And I decided to stand in front of the women without a written speech, talk from my heart as the Holy Spirit directs me and let the chips fall where they may.

Driving to the event, I did think over a few words to start my talk with. Coming up with an opening did help me so I did not feel nervous about the event. When I arrived, I was warmly greeted and hugged by a friend who was also presenting, and this gave me the final boost of confidence I needed to walk into the room—and I knew *I was there for a reason.*

Someone needed to hear my story so she can be assured she is not alone, and that she can heal and move on to be the best version of herself.

As I spoke to the women that night about my past and what I had overcome, not one of them was looking down at their phone bored or yawning. They cared about me and wanted to know where I had been and where I was going. They clapped when I finished, thanked me for sharing my story and made me feel worthy and whole, deserving of love and acceptance.

I am going to make a difference in the world one person at a time with God's help. The dreams God has written on my heart are inspiring me to shine on; I move forward enjoying the ride!

Notes

Unless otherwise indicated, scriptures are taken from the Life Application Study Bible, New International version, "NIV." Copyright 1988, 1989, 1990, 1991, 1993, 1996, 2004, 2005 by Tyndale House Publishers, Inc. Wheaton, IL 60189, All Rights Reserved.

Chapter 1 – The First Telling of My Story
1. *Grit: the Power of Passion and Perseverance* by Angela Duckworth, Scribner An Imprint of Simon & Schuster, Inc. NY, NY 2016

Chapter 7 – Health and Addiction
1. *Sugar Savvy* by Kathie "High Voltage" Dolgin, The Reader's Digest Association, Inc., New York, NY/Montreal, 2014
2. *The Gabriel Method* by Jon Gabriel, Atria Books A Division of Simon & Schuster, Inc., New York, NY, 2008
3. *Good Sugar, Bad Sugar* by Allen Carr, Arcturus Publishing Limited, London, 2016
4. Matthew 28:18-20

Chapter 8 – Light in the Darkness
1. Jeremiah 29:11
2. John 3:16
3. John 2:1-11
4. Matthew 4:19
5. *Twenty-Four Hours a Day*, Hazelden Foundation, Revised Edition 1975

6. James 1:17
7. Psalm 118:22

Chapter 10 – Racing Toward Joy

1. Psalm 81:10

Acknowledgments

I thank my mother. She has been my cheerleader my whole life and has always done her best for her children. Her mother died four days after her tenth birthday, which had an enormous impact on her life. She's always helped others and loved God more than anyone I know. She always instilled the importance of believing in God and His Son Jesus.

Secondly, I thank my husband who has painstakingly listened to every detail, regarding what I should and should not include in this book. I was always bouncing ideas off of him. And when I was in doubt, he would always say the right thing to get me back on track. I love him more than he'll ever know. I always say that he's my fixer-upper husband, but truth be told, I too was in the fix-up business. We're a match truly made in heaven, convinced that God put us together as soul mates. Yes, I made a lot of mistakes and I took the long way around to find him, but thanks be to God that I did find him in the end!

There is a long list of people that helped me in one way or another. Some people said a word or sentence that was exactly what I needed to hear at the time. Others encouraged me at a time when I needed it most.

My editors, Cole Nelson, Amy Quale, and Connie Anderson gave great advice on content, grammar, and format which was way out of my league. I am very thankful to each of you for your input because without it, this book would not be as readable.

I thank my talented, artistic daughter, Lacey Winchester, for her inspiring chapter illustrations and for her cover design collaboration with Sue Stein who also arranged the book formatting.

To my beta readers, I appreciated every word of advice you gave me. I thank you for taking the time to read my words and providing honest input.

I never knew how many people were needed to write a book until now! Thank you everyone for sharing your skills and talents with me. It truly made this journey impactful, healing, and fun for me.

Author's Bio:

Leslie Jackson has learned to embrace challenges and feels they are learning experiences that have ultimately molded her into a better person. She spends her leisure time racing her car on the dirt track, driving her motorcycle, reading books and hanging out with her beloved grand-kids, family, and friends. She lives in the country near Menomonie, Wisconsin, and has been married to her soulmate for 15 years and counting. Their three kids flew the coop leaving an empty nest so they filled it with two Great Danes, one Chinese Crested, and one Chihuahua.

Facebook: *LeslieJacksonAuthor/*
YouTube: *Lady Racing*
LinkedIn: *www.linkedin.com/in/ladyracing/*
Instagram: *ladyracing_com/*

For additional resources, please visit: *www.LadyRacing.com*
Or email: Leslie@LadyRacing.com

www.ingramcontent.com/pod-product-compliance
Lightning Source LLC
Chambersburg PA
CBHW031127080526
44587CB00011B/1140